A Journey to Healing After Emotional Abuse

T0151639

Caroline Abbott

Clovercroft Publishing

A Journey to Healing After Emotional Abuse

©2015 by Caroline Abbott

Published by Clovercroft Publishing, Franklin, Tennessee

Published in association with Larry Carpenter of Christian Book Services, LLC
www.christianbookservices.com

Unless otherwise noted, Scripture is taken from the HOLY BIBLE, NEW INTERNATIONAL VERSION®. Copyright © 1973, 1978, 1984, 2011 by Biblica, Inc.® Used by permission. All rights reserved worldwide.

Cover Design by Durand Robinson

Interior Layout Design by Suzanne Lawing

Edited by Robert Irvin

Printed in the United States of America

978-1-942557-19-7

Do not gloat over me, my enemy!
Though I have fallen, I will rise.
Though I sit in darkness,
the Lord will be my light.

—MICAH 7:8

DEDICATION

To the survivors of emotional abuse I've had the privilege to know and work with. You have inspired me with your stories of survival, courage, and hope. I pray this book will inspire you to strive for the healing you desire and deserve. May you feel God's love and peace as you read.

To my second husband. Your unconditional love has taught me much about Jesus' love for us, and guided me along my journey to healing.

CONTENTS

TERMINOLOGY

This book is written primarily for women who have been abused by and have left their male intimate partners. Many of the principles would be the same for a man who had been abused by a female intimate partner, or if the abuser and victim were of the same sex. To make this book easier to read, and to maintain focus, I will refer to the abuser as "he" and the victim as "she."

For those readers who have left their abusers, the proper terminology should be "former abusers." To prevent the need to say "former abuser" every time one is mentioned, a former abuser will simply be called abuser.

In this book, the term "pastor" is used for the leader of a church. Churches may call their leaders "minister," "priest," "father," or "rabbi" (in Messianic congregations).

Whenever names are used, they have been changed to protect the anonymity of victims of abuse.

FOREWORD

Thank God you have found the strength and courage to leave the emotionally abusive relationship that bound you. Now what? You may have already done the hard physical work of setting up a new life—finding a new home, new job, or church. But now comes the challenging emotional work of processing all you have experienced so you can move forward to a healthier you.

In these pages, Caroline shares her story of healing and provides hope as she outlines the process of thriving after abuse. As a psychotherapist, it has been my honor to walk alongside many women as they strive to work through their pain, often while providing support to their children. I have watched my clients struggle to process the pain of the past, live in the moment, and plan for their promising future. This book provides you with practical ideas on how to do all three.

A Journey to Healing provides you with a blueprint as you remember and forgive hurts of the past while setting up boundaries and healthy habits for your new path. As she did in her first book, *A Journey through Emotional Abuse*, Caroline shares helpful information and suggestions on how to protect and nurture yourself. In addition, she provides an opportunity at the end of each chapter to ask yourself insightful questions. I encourage you to sit with these questions and search your heart for honest answers. Do not rush; instead, reflect well. It is in the contemplative moments of applying these concepts and asking yourself the difficult questions that God often speaks words of healing and peace.

This book will also be helpful for those who are seeking to support you through this time of adjustment. It may be difficult for some of your friends and family to understand the extent of your pain. They may need information to be able to see things from your perspective or help you navigate the emotional roller coaster that is trauma. You may struggle to find concise explanations for your feelings while you are experiencing them. This book may give you the words you need to help your loved ones gain insight into this chapter of your life.

Healing is a longer and more arduous journey than we would like. But the journey is well worth the effort. Safety, peace, and contentment can be gained along the way. May God bless and direct your heart and mind as you work through the trauma of the past so you can find freedom in the hope of your future.

—AMY CRAIG, LICENSED PROFESSIONAL COUNSELOR
DENVER, COLORADO

ACKNOWLEDGMENTS

Thank you to Amy Craig, LPC, who went over every word to make sure I was giving sound counseling advice. Your additions, comments, and changes were invaluable.

Thank you to Durand Robinson for designing the cover, and for helping me identify my goals not only for the book, but also in ongoing ministry to emotional abuse survivors.

Thank you to the many counselors and support group leaders who have helped me on my journey to healing. I wouldn't be here without you.

Thank you to Bob Irvin, who helped me shorten the book to a reasonable size, and made my words sound good. Every author needs a good editor!

Thank you to my Lord and Savior, Jesus, for walking with me on my personal journey to healing, as well as during the writing of the book. You lift me up on wings like eagles.

INTRODUCTION

Someone once said, "It's hard to look for the light when you're lost in darkness." I have found healing from abuse can feel as if I am lost in the darkness. Other times, I feel wonderful, and I barely remember the dark times.

I was married for twenty years to an abusive man who claimed to be a Christian. Because of my faith, I took my vow to remain married until "death do us part" very seriously. My goal was to remain married no matter the cost to myself. As a result, I tried to ignore his abusive actions for many years. When my life became unbearable, I was finally honest with myself. I searched for a definition of abuse, and realized I was being abused. I hired a lawyer, petitioned a judge for a restraining order against my husband, and had him removed from my home.

We fought a contentious divorce. My church's leadership did not support me, causing me additional pain. My first book, *A Journey through Emotional Abuse: From Bondage to Freedom*, tells the story of my journey from denying I was being abused through the end of my divorce. I wrote it to help other Christian women experiencing abuse in their marriages, and also to help with my own healing. When I began helping former abuse victims via Facebook and my website, I realized other women were struggling with healing from the abuse they had suffered, just as I was. Hence, the idea for this book was born.

I took many years to heal from the abuse I suffered. I discovered my road to healing wasn't a straight line from A to Z. Instead, it seemed to happen at random. You may find your road to healing will also happen randomly. Because of this, I recommend you read the chapters I present in whatever order you need. Give yourself the freedom to walk the road to healing in the order that seems best to you.

No matter which chapters you read first, I recommend you do some journaling to help during your healing process. Recent psychological studies have proven that directed writing can help people make sense of their traumatic life experiences.[1] This is because the brain stores traumatic experiences differently than other experiences, not necessarily observing a beginning, middle, and end. Writing about your trauma helps put your experiences into linear form, organizing them in a way the brain can process.

How you write doesn't matter; neither does your grammar or how nice your handwriting looks. No one need see what you write except you. You can type it or handwrite it. You can buy a lovely bound journal—or staple some lined paper together. None of these differences matter. What matters is that you write down your feelings and thoughts. If you write your answers to the questions I ask at the end of every chapter, this will help your healing process as well.

As you read, you may feel strong emotions, such as anger, depression, or guilt. These emotions are normal for someone who has survived emotional abuse. If you struggle handling your emotions, or you become afraid for yourself or others, please seek the help of a professional counselor, or call for emergency help—dial 911 in the United States—immediately. If you find you feel a mild amount of stress as you read, consider doing one or more of the relaxation exercises I describe in Chapter 3 before you read.

Emotional abuse causes trauma. Our trauma will not magically disappear; it must be healed. I believe the only way to truly heal is to turn to the author of healing, Jesus. Perhaps your abuser claimed to be a Christian, or other Christians have hurt you. You may feel betrayed by Christians or by God, and you feel distant from Him. As a result, you may not want to turn to Him for healing. This is understandable given the pain you've experienced. After all, God could have prevented your abuse, but for some reason, He allowed it. Part of your healing will be looking at why this has happened and why God didn't prevent it.

Healing is a process. You will never "arrive," but being abused does not destine you to a life of trauma and misery. You can learn much along the journey, and you can live a productive, happy life after abuse. Your abuse is in your past. You do not need to be a victim for the rest of your life. Instead, you are a survivor.

If you struggle with strong emotions while reading this book, seek professional help, or call 911.

God loves you and cares for you. He wants your life, which was broken by the sinful actions of someone who claimed to love you, brought to restoration. God is the God of redemption! If you let Him, He will help you heal your brokenness.

Through God's inspiration, Isaiah wrote these words in Isaiah 61:

> *The Spirit of the Sovereign Lord is on me,*
> *because the Lord has anointed me*
> *to proclaim good news to the poor.*
> *He has sent me to bind up the brokenhearted,*
> *to proclaim freedom for the captives*
> *and release from darkness for the prisoners,*
> *to proclaim the year of the Lord's favor*
> *and the day of vengeance of our God,*
> *to comfort all who mourn,*
> *and provide for those who grieve in Zion—*
> *to bestow on them a crown of beauty*
> *instead of ashes,*
> *the oil of joy*
> *instead of mourning,*
> *and a garment of praise*
> *instead of a spirit of despair.*
> *They will be called oaks of righteousness,*
> *a planting of the Lord*
> *for the display of his splendor.*
> *They will rebuild the ancient ruins*
> *and restore the places long devastated;*
> *they will renew the ruined cities*
> *that have been devastated for generations.*
> *Strangers will shepherd your flocks;*
> *foreigners will work your fields and vineyards.*
> *And you will be called priests of the Lord,*
> *you will be named ministers of our God.*
> *You will feed on the wealth of nations,*
> *and in their riches you will boast.*
> *Instead of your shame*
> *you will receive a double portion, and instead of disgrace*
> *you will rejoice in your inheritance.*
> *And so you will inherit a double portion in your land,*
> *and everlasting joy will be yours.*
> *"For I, the Lord, love justice; I hate robbery and wrongdoing.*

In my faithfulness I will reward my people
and make an everlasting covenant with them.
Their descendants will be known among the nations
and their offspring among the peoples.
All who see them will acknowledge
that they are a people the Lord has blessed."
I delight greatly in the Lord; my soul rejoices in my God.
For he has clothed me with garments of salvation
and arrayed me in a robe of his righteousness,
as a bridegroom adorns his head like a priest,
and as a bride adorns herself with her jewels.
For as the soil makes the sprout come up
and a garden causes seeds to grow,
so the Sovereign Lord will make righteousness
and praise spring up before all nations.

I love these words of healing and blessing. Please allow me to come alongside you in your journey toward healing. From my own life, I know you can experience joy after being emotionally abused.

—CAROLINE ABBOTT

CHAPTER 1

Reflect on the Abuse You've Suffered

The Spirit of the Sovereign Lord is on me,
because the Lord has anointed me
to proclaim good news to the poor.

—ISAIAH 61:1

No one should have to experience the heartache of being abused, especially by someone they love and who claims to love them. You may be surprised by your conflicting feelings. No matter how long you have been apart from you abuser, you may be feeling:

- Terrified
- Angry, resentful
- Guilty, ashamed, stupid
- Relieved, free, hopeful, joyful, peaceful
- Confused, lost, empty, numb, frozen
- Like you miss him and want him back; heartbroken and lonely
- Worthy, able to think with clarity
- Destroyed, worthless, depressed
- Exhausted, drained, overwhelmed
- Reborn, like yourself for the first time in years.

Having conflicting feelings is not unusual since your abuser worked to make you feel confused about your thoughts and feelings.

Many people picture physical beatings when they think about domestic abuse. But being physically hurt is only one type of abuse. The main dynamic of an abusive relationship is that the abuser wants power and control over his victim. He will use any method to gain this power and control. If your abuser was able to keep you in line by calling you names (verbal abuse), that would be his main tool. He might have used emotional abuse, making you feel alone by isolating you from family and friends, or withholding affection from you, or giving you the silent treatment. He might have kept you trapped in the relationship by telling you the Bible says you have to submit to him in everything, even when he treated you disrespectfully. This was spiritual abuse. Perhaps he used financial abuse, forbidding you to work, or keeping control of all your money. He might have sexually abused you, forcing you to have sex against your will, forbidding you to use birth control, or making you get an abortion. He might have tried to make you think you were going crazy by psychologically abusing you.

> An abuser's goal is to gain power and control over his victim. He will use whatever tool he can to accomplish these things.

Here is an example of psychological abuse, an action called *gaslighting*: he moves your keys from where you always put them. When you can't find them, he seems empathetic, and helps you look through the house for them. After quite a while, he finds them in the place he previously hid them. He might play this game with your purse in two weeks, the papers you need for a presentation next month. Each time he "helps" you find them, then seems concerned you might be losing your mind. Later when he does something that is clearly abusive, if you challenge him, he will remind you how often you "lose" things, so perhaps you don't really understand what is happening, or maybe you don't remember it clearly.

The examples I've given are only a few of the ways your abuser might have treated you in order to control you. (For a more extensive list of tactics your abuser might have used, see Appendix B.)

The terms *verbal, psychological,* and *spiritual abuse* are often used interchangeably with emotional abuse. Victims who have suffered from both physical and nonphysical abuse often say the nonphysical or emotional abuse took longer to heal. This is because bruises, cuts, and broken bones heal quicker than the longer-lasting hits to a victim's self-worth, which is injured by a loved one emotionally abusing her. As a result, this book will focus on healing from emotional abuse.

Another characteristic about domestic abuse is that it goes in cycles. At times, your abuser behaved like I described above. This is called the *explosive* stage[2] of abuse. But after that, he might have behaved wonderfully, much like he did when you first met. He might have bought you flowers, took you on special dates, and told you how much he loved you. Unfortunately, this wasn't the end of the abuse, only a stage of the abuse cycle called the *honeymoon* or *hearts and flowers* stage. Your abuser behaved this way to keep you from leaving him. No one wants to live with a person who is cruel all the time.

> Victims of abuse often say the emotional abuse they suffered took longer to heal than the physical abuse.

The honeymoon stage may have lasted a few hours, weeks, months, or years. It was usually followed by a buildup of tension, a period in which you felt like you were walking on eggshells. This part of the cycle is called the *tension-building stage*. In this stage, you probably did anything you could not to upset your abuser. You may have told him anything he wanted to hear, and withheld any information, feelings, or thoughts that might have made him angry.

In my first marriage, the honeymoon stage was wonderful, and I occasionally did forget some of the awful things he had done. This forgetting made it hard for me to be honest with myself about what was really happening. Did you find this to be true in your abusive relationship? Many abusers are so good at the honeymoon stage that they can convince their partners they've actually changed. This isn't unusual. He may have really acted like he had changed. He may have behaved kindly toward you, told you how much he loved you, considered your ideas, allowed you to visit your friends and family, get a job, and more. Sadly, this didn't mean he had really changed. Once you leave your abuser, he may still try to get you to return to him by going into the honeymoon stage of the abuse cycle.

Thinking of the abuser's behaviors as the repetitive, round-and-round cycle of abuse diagrammed by the Bridges Domestic and Sexual Violence Support Group (figure above) can be helpful.[3] It describes the three emotions that kept the cycle going: love, hope, and fear:

- You **loved** your partner, and the relationship had its good points.

- You **hoped** the behavior would change because the relationship didn't start out like this.

- You **feared** your partner would follow through with threats he made against you or your loved ones.

Some abusive relationships don't follow the honeymoon/tension-building/explosion pattern. Some don't have a honeymoon stage. These abusers move from the explosive stage directly into the tension-building stage. Other abusers are so unpredictable they sometimes skip the tension-building stage and move from the honeymoon stage right into the next explosion. Perhaps you're wondering why you never recognized this abusive pattern before, and why you stayed in your abusive relationship so long. Maybe you are angry with your loved ones for not seeing the pattern and trying harder to protect you. You aren't alone. Abusers are wily and manipulative; their tactics are hard to spot.

Your abuser's goal was to lower your self-esteem so he could gain control over you. Did you begin to feel less attractive over time, less worthy of his love? Did you begin to think even his abuse was your fault? Maybe if you had done something more perfectly, or if you hadn't said . . . *then* he wouldn't have called you names, broken your treasured items, made you feel worthless.

Why did he want to treat you this way? In *Why Does He DO That? Inside the Minds of Angry and Controlling Men*,[4] Lundy Bancroft says that in the mind of an abuser, he:

- liked being in control

- convinced himself it was OK to act this way toward you

- got you to do whatever he wanted by this behavior.

In *It's My Life Now*, Meg Kennedy Dugan and Roger Hock opine that your abuser worked to lower your self-esteem to guarantee you would stay with him.[5] Perhaps your abuser was able to convince you that you were ugly, fat, stupid, and no one (but him) would ever want you or love you. He was doing you a favor by staying by your side, right? *Wrong!* You are not ugly, fat, or stupid. It is not true that no one will ever want or love you. For starters, the God of the universe loved you so much He was willing to leave Heaven, come to earth as a squalling baby in a smelly barn, live a life as a nobody, and die a humiliating, painful death, *for you.* Romans 5:8 says:

> *But God demonstrates his own love for us in this:*
> *While we were still sinners, Christ died for us.*

I pray you will regain your self-esteem, and as you read this book that you further realize how wonderful you are and how very much you are loved. Please read on, my friend!

Lundy Bancroft says your abuser behaves this way because he:

- likes being in control

- believes it's OK to treat you this way

- gets what he wants

A Drink of Water for the Journey

"I have a message from God in my heart
concerning the sinfulness of the wicked:
There is no fear of God before their eyes.
In their own eyes they flatter themselves
too much to detect or hate their sin.
The words of their mouths are wicked and deceitful;
they fail to act wisely or do good.
Even on their beds they plot evil;
they commit themselves to a sinful course
and do not reject what is wrong.
Your love, Lord, reaches to the heavens,
your faithfulness to the skies . . .
How priceless your unfailing love, O God!
People take refuge in the shadow of your wings.

—PSALM 36:1-5, 7

1. Make a list of the feelings you had when you first left your abusive relationship, and how you feel now. All feelings are acceptable; none are wrong.

2. Which abusive behaviors did your abuser use to control you? Can you think of others not listed here?

3. Did your abuse happen in obvious stages and cycles? Did you hide parts of your life from your abuser to prevent the explosive stage from happening?

4. Did your abuser pretend his abusive behavior was your fault, or never happened? Did you ever feel confused about what was happening? Describe what that felt like.

5. Do you believe your partner abused you to get what he wanted in the relationship, and that part of what he wanted was to lower your self-esteem to make you stay with him?

6. What lies did your abuser tell you so you would think you were unworthy of his or anyone else's love? Do you believe you are worthy of God's love? Do you believe God *does* love you? Why or why not?

CHAPTER 2

Set Boundaries with Your Abuser for Your Physical and Emotional Safety

. . . to proclaim freedom for the captives . . .

—Isaiah 61:1

Setting boundaries with your abuser, even after you have separated from him, can be difficult, but I believe it is necessary for your healing and future happiness. I found setting boundaries with my ex difficult after we separated. During my marriage, he used emotional, psychological, and verbal abuse to break my self-confidence, which allowed him to slowly gain power and control over me. During the last years of my marriage, I followed his every demand; still, I didn't fully realize I was being abused, only that I was deeply unhappy.

One day he asked me to tell our children he had never abused me. I began looking for a definition of abuse and realized he had been abusing me for many years. My spirit balked at the idea of lying to our children, so I refused to do it. Secretly, I visited my local women's crisis center and found a lawyer. Together with my lawyer, we petitioned the court for a restraining order. Later that day, a process server delivered the restraining order to him.

Though I had demonstrated courage in removing him from our home, I hadn't yet learned to change the dynamics of our relationship. He continued to try to control me any way he could, and I had little self-confidence. He first tried to reconcile with me by going into the honeymoon stage of the cycle of violence. Though my restraining order forbid using other people to contact me, he called my parents, our pastors, and our children to try to regain control over me. He told them how much he loved me, that he had been wrong, and he was going to change. This was from a man who had not spoken to me for the entire previous year except to rage at me.

Though he had broken my trust continually for years, I was confident the Lord didn't want me to continue accepting his abuse, and I had no love left for him; his seemingly loving behavior caused me to stumble. I began to second-guess my decision to leave him . . . had I made a mistake? Was he really willing to change? Had I given up too soon? Perhaps this has happened to you.

Does this mean we are weak? *No.* It does mean we have experienced emotional abuse at the hands of someone we once thought we loved, and may still love. We also thought he loved us, and we built a life with him. In my case, I had been married to him for twenty years, had children with him, and had gone to church with him. Everyone I knew thought of me as his wife and the mother of his children. My status at church came from being his wife. Suddenly, in one day, my reputation and self-worth were wiped away, and my children were without their father. Fortunately, I wasn't dependent on him financially, as most abused women are.

Given that you have so much to lose when you leave your abuser, and your self-esteem is probably low, is it surprising you might be second-guessing your decision to leave?

> Abuse victims leave and then return to their abusers, on average, seven times. This shows how unlikely it is that their abuser will make real changes, *and* how difficult it is for the victim to leave and not return.

Abuse victims leave and then return to their abusers, on average, seven times before they finally leave and don't return. The fact that they continue leaving demonstrates how unlikely it is their abuser will make substantial changes in his behavior. However, the fact that they return so many times demonstrates how difficult it is for them to leave and not return.

In addition to our abuser, we have another foe that doesn't want us to succeed in our healing. Satan will use:

- the abuse you've experienced
- your feelings of low self-worth
- the love you have felt for your abuser, and
- how much you have to lose

to cause you to doubt your decision to leave your abuser. Ephesians 6:12 says:

> *For our struggle is not against flesh and blood, but against the rulers, against the authorities, against the powers of this dark world and against the spiritual forces of evil in the heavenly realms.*

The apostle Paul, by inspiration of the Holy Spirit, correctly identified our real enemy as we fight for healing: the spiritual forces of evil in the heavenly realms, Satan and his demons. They will use the words and actions of our abuser to try to keep us in bondage.

Because of the difficulty former victims have in leaving their abusers, I recommend you set boundaries around any continued relationship you might have with yours. As long as he continues to be part of your life, you will find it difficult to begin your journey toward healing.

What Exactly Are Boundaries?

In their book *Boundaries: When to Say Yes, When to Say No to Take Control of Your Life*, Dr. Henry Cloud and Dr. John Townsend[6] explain that relational boundaries show where I end and someone else begins, just as the boundary lines in my yard show where my property ends and my neighbor's yard begins. I am only responsible to mow, fertilize, and water the grass on my property, not that of my neighbor's.

Relational boundaries are like the boundary of the skin on my body. My skin is designed to keep good things in my body and to keep harmful things out of it. So, too, a relational boundary helps me keep in the good things in my life (happiness, joy, and peace, for example) and keep the bad things (pain, abuse, sorrow, and similar negatives) out. Unfortunately, while I was being abused, I didn't use boundaries to protect myself. I kept the bad inside: I allowed pain, abuse, and sorrow to exist in my abusive relationship, and I kept the good (happiness, joy, and peace) that I might have received from friends and family outside. Perhaps you had a similar experience. As I learned to use boundaries effectively, I began to switch these patterns so that the bad flowed out and the good flowed in.

Boundaries rely on the law of sowing and reaping. Galatians 6:7 says:

> Do not be deceived: God cannot be mocked.
> A man reaps what he sows.

In the natural world, if a farmer plants poor seed, he receives a poor crop. During my abusive relationship, however, my abuser planted poor seed (poor treatment of me) and received a good crop (more loving treatment) in return. The worse he treated me, the better I behaved in return. I did this to try to protect myself from his abuse, but it didn't work. His abuse only escalated. Finally, I set the ultimate boundary with him; I got a restraining order and had him legally removed from my home.

Now that you have left your abuser, you have also set the ultimate boundary with him, and your abuser has reaped what he has sown, the loss of your relationship. By leaving your abusive relationship, you have created a very distinct boundary line with your abuser. You have said, "My life exists on *this* side of the line, and your life exists on *that* side of the line."

Learning to reset your boundaries takes practice. You may set your boundaries too tightly and keep everyone out, or too loosely and find others taking advantage of you. Do you have someone in your life who is good at setting boundaries? Perhaps you can use this person as a role model and watch how she (or he) sets boundaries with others.

> We train people how to treat us. If we allow people to treat us badly, they will.

Protecting Your Physical Safety

The first question to ask yourself is: "Are you afraid your abuser might physically harm you, your children, your family, your pets, or your property?"

People may say you should no longer be afraid of your abuser. After all, you are out of the relationship, right? *Wrong!* The most dangerous time for an abuse victim is when she leaves the relationship. Your abuser has lost something very valuable to him—a person he can control. He views you as something that belongs to him, and he will probably be angry when it's gone.

This doesn't mean you need to live in fear, but it does mean making every effort to keep yourself safe is wise. You may feel so relieved to be free that you are not concerned about your safety. Ask yourself if people who know you well are concerned. If so, this could be a sign you should be as well. Sometimes the opposite is true. Family and friends who are uneducated about domestic violence may not be good judges of violence risks; they may think you are safe now, but you are still frightened.

Your local women's crisis center is a good resource for helping you discern your risk level. Contact the National Domestic Violence Hotline at 1-800-799-SAFE (7233) or 1-800-787-3224 (TTY) to find the nearest women's crisis center.[7] Domestic violence advocates at your local crisis center can complete a danger assessment[8] for you. The Danger Assessment Instrument is a tool created by Dr. Jacquelyn C. Campbell that puts a numeric score to your risk of being killed by your abuser. (Recently, this tool was made into a phone app called the One Love My Plan app.[9] You can use this app to discern your danger level.) I recommend you contact a domestic violence advocate if you are at all concerned about your safety.

> A domestic violence advocate can help you discern your level of risk from your abuser and whether you should get a civil restraining order.

Once you know your score, you will be better able to discern whether you should take extreme precautions or whether you should simply be mindful of your safety.

What Is a Civil Restraining Order?

If your risk score is high, you might consider getting a civil restraining order (sometimes called a protection order). A judge will issue this order if you can prove you have reason to be afraid of your partner. The initial order is usually temporary and lasts between two to four weeks. Your partner is not in the courtroom when the initial temporary order is issued.

The temporary order will have language similar to the following, stating your abuser is not allowed to:

- harass, stalk, injure, intimidate, threaten, molest, or use any physical force against you

- contact you, nor is he allowed to contact you through any third party except an attorney.

In addition, he must:

- keep a physical distance of 100 yards (or some distance specified by the judge) away from you

- not enter a home, workplace, school, or any other place you might be.

Your children may or may not be added to the order, depending on whether the judge feels they also need protection.

The temporary order will be fairly easy to obtain. A process server or law enforcement officer must serve it to the restrained person (your abuser). If your abuser does any of the actions listed on the restraining order, the protected person (you) is allowed to call the police, and if the police believe he has in fact broken the restraining order, he can be arrested.

A permanent restraining order is more difficult to get. Before the temporary order expires,[10] both parties must appear before the judge, and each gets to explain what has happened from their perspective. In cases of emotional abuse, and even in cases of minor physical abuse, a judge will rarely order a permanent restraining order. This usually requires documented proof of repeated physical abuse. However, if your abuser has broken the temporary order and you have called the police, you will find it easier to get a permanent order. In many states, the restrained person can petition the court to have the permanent restraining order removed every four years. The result is entirely up to the judge.

> If you have received a restraining order, never try contacting the restrained person. Doing so appears to the court as if you are not really afraid of him.

Note that if you are the protected party, you should never try to contact the restrained person, except in the ways the restraining order allows. For example, you may be allowed to email your abuser concerning scheduling the children. Other than this, contacting him will appear to the court as though you are not really afraid of him.

Should You Try to Get a Civil Restraining Order?

A civil restraining order can be very helpful if your abuser is the type of person who would follow such an order. The sad truth, however, is that many abusive men refuse to follow the restraining order until they are arrested for breaking it. After that, many follow the order because their abusive actions finally cause them discomfort.

However, some abusers become much more violent when a restraining order has been issued. They are not deterred by the threat of going to jail. In fact, they see it as a challenge, and they may behave much worse than if you simply left. For this type of man, getting a restraining order does not help—it only makes things worse. You are the best judge of your abuser's potential reaction to such a step. Your local women's crisis center can help you think through what is best for your circumstances.

> You are the best judge of your abuser's potential reaction. Will he abide by the restraining order, or see it as a challenge?

If you do decide to get a restraining order, be prepared to enforce it. A restraining order will do you no good if you are unwilling to call the police when your abuser does something the order has forbidden him to do. You may struggle with this. I know I did. A few weeks after the court granted my restraining order, I went to the gym to work out with my kids. My husband came into the gym and began working out 10 feet from me, though our restraining order said he must keep 100 yards away! I should have called the police at that moment, but I was too embarrassed. Instead, I walked up to him and said, "You are not allowed to be here according to the restraining order." He looked smug and answered, "My lawyer said I could." I went to the locker room and called my lawyer. Her advice? "Call the police." I wish I had, but I did not have enough self-esteem to make the call.

Whether or not you have a restraining order, you will want to keep your safety in mind. Be aware of your surroundings. Ask a domestic violence advocate to help you come up with a safety plan. Some things to consider:

• What will you do if your abuser enters your home?

- What will you do if he shows up at your workplace? Consider speaking to your boss or your human resources department proactively to ask if your workplace has any policies in place that can help you stay safe. For example, you can move your desk away from the entrance, have a security guard walk you to and from your car, or change your shifts so your ex doesn't know when you'll be there.

- What will you do if he finds you at another public place, such as a store or movie theater?

- Do not share your plan with the general public, but do include close family members, your children, and neighbors regarding your intentions.

- Do not be embarrassed to call the police if you feel afraid of your abuser, even if you don't have a restraining order—better safe than sorry.

If You Still Must Have Contact with Him

If you must have some contact with your abuser because you have children you must parent together, try to limit your exposure to him as much as possible. You can try these ideas:

1. **Change your locks**: Once you are separated, he no longer lives in your home; therefore, he should not have a key. This is a reasonable boundary line for you to insist on. I recommend changing the locks on every door in your home. If you have a garage, change the code used to program the opener. If you have an alarm system, change the alarm code and the password. You should also change the key to your car if possible, and any storage unit you might have. Keep your windows shut and locked, and your alarm system armed at all times. Keeping him out of your life and his negative words out of your head will be much easier if he is not allowed in your home.

> Keeping your abuser out of your life and his negative words out of your head will be much easier if he is not allowed in your home.

Your children may make this harder. They might invite their father into your home when he picks them up or drops them off. Or they may beg you to include him in family get-togethers. Explain to them that he is their father, and always will be, but he no longer lives in your home, and you are no longer a couple. Allowing him in your home gives them false hope, and doing so allows him power over you that you are trying to regain.

One former abuse victim I know gave in to the pleading of her children to allow her soon-to-be ex-husband into her home to open Christmas presents with her and her kids. He was there for one hour. She was distressed in the following days when he began emotionally abusing her again. Before Christmas he had rarely contacted her. After Christmas, he began texting her several times a day, getting involved in minor disputes between her kids, and saying he was going to come over and "fix" the problems she was "unable to handle." She vowed to never allow him in her home again. The hour he spent there undid several months of hard work she had put in to set proper boundaries.

2. **Cancel your bank accounts:** I recommend you cancel any jointly owned bank or credit card accounts as soon as possible. He could easily empty all of your shared accounts at any moment. One friend's ex-husband pretended to be very friendly while they were going through their divorce. Without warning, he took all of the money from their joint accounts and closed them. Closing or changing the passwords on any individual accounts you own is also wise since he might try to empty those accounts as well.

3. **Change your phone numbers and social media accounts:** Your abuser may continue to contact you through your phone(s). Unless you absolutely must speak to him, you may want to change your cell, home, and even work phone numbers (speak to your work supervisor). If you decide not to change your numbers, you can block his number from ringing yours. You may choose to change your email, Facebook, Twitter, and other social media accounts, or block him from those accounts. I strongly recommend you change your passwords so he cannot sabotage you or read personal messages you might receive.

4. **Limit co-parenting conversations:** Though you may be forced to co-parent with him, this does not mean he should contact you 24 hours a day. You might try to limit your contact to text messages that only concern scheduling for the children. If your abuser takes advantage of this and sends you text messages about other things, such as trying to reconcile with you, speaking abusively toward you, or threatening you— really, for any reason other than scheduling the children—you may want

to block him from your phones completely and only use email communication. Acquire a new email address for everyone else, and use your old address to communicate with him. This way, you will only need to look at it when you decide to. He could email you ten times a day, and you might decide to look at this account once a day or once a week. This will relieve you from being bombarded by his correspondence if they are sent many times each day.

> If you have children with your abuser and must parent together, this does not mean he should contact you 24 hours a day.

When you do look at his emails, try not to take his emotional abuse seriously. Skim the emails for content that's important to you, and teach yourself to ignore the rest. You will likely find this difficult at first, but you will find it easier over time as you become less emotionally tied to him.

I learned this lesson the hard way. My ex-husband was a great arguer. During our marriage, I never won an argument, because he could "logically" talk me out of any position I held, no matter how well thought out. When we first separated, he would attempt to talk me out of things I wanted to do for our kids, like purchasing a bicycle for one of them.

I read his controlling emails and got angry. Then I would make the mistake of trying to explain myself. He would shoot back an email telling me I was wrong and stupid. This would make me more furious, so I would send back an angry reply. This could go on indefinitely. I eventually realized that I would never win an argument with him, nor would I get him to see my side of a situation. I was wasting my time, and I was giving him what he wanted—my attention. I began asking myself, "Why am I allowing him to ruin my days with his abuse when I am divorcing him to get away from it?"

A friend of mine, who had been through this with her ex-husband, gave me excellent advice. She said, "Only respond to the emails you absolutely must, such as questions about schedule changes for the children. Don't defend yourself, your decisions, and your actions—even as they apply to the children. This only adds fuel to his fire and keeps you engaged with him. Your goal is to disengage. If you feel you must respond, give a one-word answer such as OK, yes, no, sure—but not a curse word. Making him angry won't help you *dis*engage with him, but will keep you tied to him."

I found this difficult at first, but finally realized the less I responded the less he emailed me, giving me a more peaceful life. One way to visualize this is to see your interaction with him like a TV show. When you argue with him, your interaction is vivid, in living color. Imagine your interactions in black and white. You are trying to drain the color out of the communication. Make it as fact-based, boring, and brief as possible.

A word of caution: abusers who tend to be violent may become enraged as you disengage. Speak to a crisis center domestic violence advocate if you are concerned for your safety.

Protect Your Emotional Safety

Just as setting physical boundaries with your abuser helps keep you physically safe, setting emotional boundaries helps keep you emotionally safe and helps you begin healing. Here are some common tactics abusers use to emotionally hurt their former partners. Once you are prepared for these potential landmines, you can guard yourself against them.

1. **He may make threats against you, your family, your property, or your pets.**
If he threatens you, take him seriously. Yes, he might threaten you just to upset you, but it's also possible he plans to carry out his threats. (Review the previous section on protecting your physical safety.)

> Take him seriously if he makes threats against you, your family, your property, or your pets.

2. **He may flaunt one or more new girlfriends.** While you may not care if he finds someone new, you *may* care, and for several reasons, including feeling jealous because you still love him; you may have heard bad things about her and worry about her influence on your kids; and you may worry about her safety, given your abuse.

If you are jealous of or dislike the new girlfriend, there is little you can do. You will have to handle these emotions as best you can without allowing them to affect your children.

If you feel compelled to warn her, carefully consider why. If you warn her because you still love him and want him for yourself, this will likely hurt you in the long run. If, however, you are sincerely afraid for her, think it through. If you warn her, and your ex finds out about it, he may come after you. If he doesn't, he will probably tell her that you are "crazy," and she will not believe you, but she may at least file this information for the future.

One of my friends told the new girlfriend she wished her luck, and suggested she take self-defense classes. The new girlfriend broke up with him three days later. Should you warn her? This is a difficult question. In reality, you are responsible only for your safety and the safety of your children, not for another adult woman. She is responsible for her own life and decisions.

3. **He may bad-mouth you to your friends, family, work acquaintances, and your church.** In fact, he probably will, and this will be painful for you. You may love his family members and consider them *your* family. Suddenly, they are no longer yours. You may have friends together as a couple who will choose to side with him, and suddenly they don't return your phone calls. If you worked together, your place of work may feel unbearable as your former work friends talk behind your back. Finally, your church family may turn its back on you, which may be the most painful loss of all, as this may feel as if God is turning His back on you. All of these are painful losses, and there is very little you can do about them. The more you try to defend yourself to these people, the more desperate you will look. People who side with an abuser will probably not change their minds no matter what you say.

I recommend you hold your head up, be as kind to them as you can, and distance yourself from the drama. You may find changing jobs and churches will be your best choice in the long run, but I don't recommend you do this immediately. Hang in there for a while and see what happens. Don't talk about him behind his back, don't defend yourself, and certainly don't seek or think about revenge. Go about your work or church duties to benefit your boss and bring honor to Jesus. People often realize over time who was the perpetrator and who was the innocent party.

4. **He may try to ruin your reputation via social media.** He may use his Facebook, Twitter, or any other social media account to bad-mouth you in a very public way. While social media can be a blessing, sometimes it can be a curse. He may post negative comments about you ten times a day. My recommendation would be to block him from all your

> If he posts anything pornographic or offensive about you on social media, report him.

social media accounts so you can't see anything he posts. Friends and pseudo-friends might tell you what he's doing, but you don't need to see it every time you get on your social media accounts. If any of your "friends" repost his posts, block them as well. The less you respond to this, the faster it will stop.

If he posts anything offensive or pornographic such as nude pictures of you, contact Facebook and Twitter and report him immediately. They will take charge of kicking him off their site.

Protecting Your Emotional Safety If You Have Children with Your Abuser

1. **When dropping off/picking up your children from visits,** he may harass you, order you around, question your parenting, or threaten you, much as he did when you were together.

2. **Or, he may return them late, or not return them at all for days or weeks.**

If he harasses you when dropping off the children more than once or twice, I recommend you find a neutral place to meet. My city has a Safe Exchange Program that provides a nonthreatening and comfortable place for children to wait for contact with the other parent while remaining under supervision of the Safe Exchange staff. You can drop off your children early and safely leave before your abuser arrives to get them. If your city doesn't have a Safe Exchange program, you may be able to use a police or fire station in a similar way. Your local women's crisis center can help you decide how best to safely set these boundaries.

> If he harasses you when exchanging your children, look for a neutral/safe place to drop off the kids.

If he doesn't return the children to you at the agreed time, you can report this to the police, your custody evaluator, or Social Services. Make sure you show them your custody agreement in writing. If he continues to do this, don't agree to change your parenting time. Keep to the agreement as much as possible, then ask the authorities to help you enforce it.

3. **He may attempt to turn the children against you by:**

a. Placing the blame for the breakup of your relationship on you. You know what really happened in your relationship with their father, and you may think it would be obvious to your children that you left the relationship because their father was treating you abusively. Your children may surprise you by siding with your abuser, especially if they see you as weak or if he convinces them he has changed, and tells them you are at fault for not re-uniting the family.

b. Refusing to discipline them, so that you look like the bad guy. Abusive parents have little interest in disciplining the children for their good. They might swing between giving harsh, abusive discipline and being extremely permissive. If your kids tell him you said no about something, he might tell them how "mean" you are and that they "don't need to do that at *his* house . . . this will be our little secret."

c. Giving them things you cannot, or things you have decided are not good for them. Often your abuser may have more income than you and may use this money to buy your children. He might take them out to eat every night or to the amusement park every weekend, while you struggle to buy enough food for all of you to eat well. You must buy them school supplies, while he is buying them the latest fashionable clothes and computer games. (Then he lets them stay up late playing the games on school nights instead of doing their homework.)

> Don't speak badly of your ex to your kids. This will only hurt all of you in the long run.

How does a good mother handle being the bad guy? It may be tempting to speak badly to your children about their father. However, I strongly recommend you don't do this. This will only lead to heartache for all of you in the long run. Why? Reasons include:

• Your abuser is your child(ren)'s parent. No matter what his faults, they see themselves in him. Perhaps they have his hair or eye color. Perhaps they talk or walk the same. If he is worthless, they will see themselves as worthless. This may not make sense to you, but this is how your children will see it.

- If you choose to bad-mouth your abuser, the children are left with two choices. They can side with you and begin telling your abuser his actions are wrong. This may open them up to his anger, and it also makes the child a parentified adult, or a child taking on the role of your emotional partner. Or if the children defend your abuser, you will feel hurt. This may cause a rift in your relationship.

- In the long run, your children will respect you if you don't bad-mouth their father. They will also begin to see his faults for themselves. On the other hand, if you do bad-mouth him, they will lose respect for you.

This doesn't mean you cannot periodically correct blatant lies your children hear from your ex. But don't spend a lot of time doing this. Work on being the bigger person.

4. **He may treat the children badly to upset you.** Abusers often see their children as objects to be used rather than as people. After all, isn't that how he treated you? Therefore, he may have little interest in being a good father. He knows you love your children and want to protect them. Because of this, he may harm them just to hurt you. This may take several forms, including: being inconsistent in their lives (such as not showing for his scheduled visits); refusing to help you with child support, or paying it inconsistently; neglecting them during his parenting time (leaving them alone, placing them in front of the TV, or ignoring them while spending time with friends or a new girlfriend); and even abusing them emotionally, physically, or sexually.

What can you do if your ex does these things?

If your ex is an inconsistent father, try to be as loving and consistent as you can. When he doesn't show up for a visit, don't wait all day for him to arrive. Have another activity planned for your kids. Try to be as positive as you can under the circumstances. Don't talk negatively about him, but don't try to invent reasons why he didn't show. Just be matter-of-fact and say truthfully that you don't know

> If your ex consistently doesn't show up for his parenting time, have other activities planned for the kids, find time for yourself another way, and find other mentors for them.

why he isn't there, then move along to the next activity.

Because you can't count on him to give you a much-needed break, plan to get time for yourself on another day. If you can afford it, hire a babysitter. If not, enlist a family member or exchange time with another single mom. Get creative. However, making time for *you* is a priority. You're worth it, and your kids need a relaxed, rested mom.

Finally, bring other, more consistent men into your children's lives. This could be family members, husbands of your friends, mentors from church, coaches, or scout troop leaders. However, keep a close eye on your children's relationships with these men. Sexual predators sometimes prey on children of single mothers, especially if they think you aren't paying attention.[11] Watch your children for signs of unease around them, or hints that they don't want to be alone with them. They needn't spend time alone with men to build strong bonds. You can spend time with your kids and other families, including other moms and kids. Your kids can learn about healthy families by watching others in action.

If your ex refuses to pay court-mandated child support, you can take him back to court. Many states will take the child support he owes out of his paycheck before he receives it. Of course, even if you represent yourself without a lawyer, it takes time and effort to go to court, time away from a job at which you need to be working. Still, you may decide it's worth the effort.

Some abusers purposely quit or lose their jobs so they don't have to pay child support. If this happens, you may find it difficult to make him pay the money he owes you. In this case, I recommend you decide to live without the money. I know this is easier for me to say than for you to do. However, if you can't make him pay you, counting on it but never receiving it will make you miserable. If you plan your life as if you will never receive it, you will be more at peace. Then, if he *does* pay you the money he owes you, it will be a bonus. You can use it for a vacation, put it toward savings, or use it for a big expense that you couldn't normally afford, like a car repair or new piece of furniture.

If you find yourself unable to make ends meet, be willing to accept help from friends, your church, or even the government. Now is not the time to be proud. You are taking care of your children, and this is just a season of your life. You will not always need to accept this help; better days are ahead.

> If you disagree with the way your ex raises your kids (and they aren't being abused or neglected), focus on giving them the best environment you can while they are with you.

If he neglects your child(ren), try to discern to what extent this is happening. If they are physically safe but he parks them in front of the television or video games while he entertains himself elsewhere, there is little you can do. You will have to deal with your own emotions about this. For example, if keeping your kids away from junk television or violent video games is important to you, this will be especially difficult. Alternatively, if your ex is spending his time having sex with the woman he cheated with during your marriage, this situation will be doubly upsetting.

How can you deal with these angry—and very understandable—emotions? Try to keep busy while your children are spending time with their father so you aren't dwelling on what they are (or aren't) doing while they are with him. Use the time to visit friends, see a movie, read a book, take a long bath—anything you enjoy.

Once the kids are back with you, try not to pepper them with questions, as this can leave them feeling as if they are tattling on their father. If they ask you questions about what their father does while they're with him, answer them with as little emotion as possible. Then try to focus on giving your children the best environment possible when they are with you.

Extremely important: if he abuses them or seriously neglects them (such as leaving young children completely alone), try your best to get proof. If you have a custody evaluator on your case, you should report this. Most authorities will do very little if a parent emotionally abuses their children. However, physical and sexual abuse *should* be taken seriously. Consider calling Social Services or the police. (I will discuss this further in Chapter 7.)

5. **He may encourage the children to harass you by:**

• passing messages to you from him

• telling you what he thinks of you

• giving you orders from him

• teaching them to disrespect you, even call you curse words

> You and your children are a new family unit. You are now the authority figure in your house and deserve respect. Their father is no longer part of the home.

- encouraging them to be abusive toward you.

How should you react if your children begin harassing you in these ways?

You and your children are creating a new family unit, of which their father is no longer a part. You are their mother and the only authority figure in your home. Remembering these things will help you. If your ex wants to give you a message, let your children know he has a way to do this: via email or text. Refuse to listen to any message they deliver to you. If they tell you anyway, don't act on the information. Remind them their father can deliver the message himself, then drop the subject. Let your children know they have many important jobs: going to school, doing homework, being a great family member, doing their chores around your house. But passing messages between their parents isn't one of their jobs.

You may also be tempted to ask the children for information about your ex or to pass information to him through them. Please resist this temptation. This will only delay your children's healing process. Though you may be intensely curious about your ex's actions, using your kids in this way will only hurt all of you in the long run.

If your children insist on telling you what dad thinks of you, you can calmly let them know that dad has a right to his opinion, but you don't want to hear it. Your ex has no right to give you orders. As the only parent in your new family, you deserve respect. You need not allow your children to treat you abusively, with disrespect, or to curse at you. (I discuss this further in Chapter 7.)

You may find your children act out most right after returning home from a visit to your ex. This transition is difficult for children of any age. Be aware this is a time they need to let their defenses down and settle back into your safe home with proper expectations—and give them an extra measure of grace.

Summary

Learning to set boundaries is often difficult, especially for a former abuse victim. This is something I still struggle with, many years after leaving my abuser. However, putting boundaries around your boundary-less abuser will help you take back your life and begin to heal from the emotional abuse he has caused you. Setting and keeping these boundaries will grow easier, and you will find yourself less emotionally attached to him as time passes.

A Drink of Water for the Journey

But mark this: There will be terrible times in the last days. People will be lovers of themselves, lovers of money, boastful, proud, abusive, disobedient to their parents, ungrateful, unholy, without love, unforgiving, slanderous, without self-control, brutal, not lovers of the good, treacherous, rash, conceited, lovers of pleasure rather than lovers of God—having a form of godliness but denying its power. Have nothing to do with such people.

—2 Timothy 3:1-5

1. How many times did you leave and then return to your abuser? Do you still struggle with wanting to return to him? Can you explain your feelings about this?

2. Are you afraid your abuser might physically harm you, your children, your family, your pets, or your property? If so, what steps have you taken (or can you take) to ensure your safety? Who can you turn to for help?

3. Has your abuser tried to contact you more often than you would like? Which of the suggestions made in this chapter might you try to prevent him from doing this?

4. What way(s) has your abuser tried to emotionally hurt you since you separated? What have you done (or could you do) to limit your emotional pain?

5. If your ex's attempts to hurt you have also hurt your child(ren), how have you handled this? Is there any way you can make this better for all of you? Watching him hurt your kid(s) is painful. How can you handle your emotions about this?

CHAPTER 3

Practice Self-Care

He has sent me to bind up the brokenhearted...

—Isaiah 61:1

What is self-care? This simply means *taking care of you*. This may be a foreign concept! For a long time your life revolved around your abuser, making *him* happy, anticipating his needs, avoiding his anger. If you're a mother, you probably now focus on the needs of your hurting children. Or, you may be taking care of your aging parents or seeing to the needs of a coworker. The idea of taking care of you may seem laughable.

You may think taking care of yourself is selfish. Many girls learn at a young age to take care of others, putting the needs of others before their own. I believe this is built into girls from birth. When my first daughter was born, I was determined not to force her into stereotypical feminine roles. I bought her a small toy truck and a little baby doll. I gave them both to her at the same time, with equal excitement. She looked at the truck and watched with disinterest as I rolled it back and forth, making "vroom, vroom" sounds. When I handed her the doll, she immediately grabbed it and pulled it to her chest. From that moment on, her doll was rarely out of her arms. She was not yet walking, but she dragged it behind her everywhere as she crawled around, as though this doll was hers and hers alone to care for. When my son was born, I gave him the same choice. He didn't even look at the doll, but loved that truck!

Given that women are born nurturers who are often trained to put the needs of others before themselves—and, if you are a woman, you have recently left an abusive relationship where his needs took precedence over *your* needs—then you must realize that learning to take care of yourself may be a challenge. However, this is an important step in your healing process. Why?

> When you take care of yourself, you can focus on healing from the abuse you've suffered, which takes time and energy.

1. You must value yourself in order to focus on your journey to healing. Healing from emotional abuse will take time and energy. It won't happen overnight, or by wishful thinking.

2. You have been through a terrible ordeal. You will need to be kind to yourself to begin making up for the cruelty you've suffered.

3. In the midst of the trauma of emotional abuse and then the stress of leaving and setting up a new household, your body can literally forget how to relax. God gave us the ability to go through hard times and to emotionally and physically carry a heavy load for a time, but our bodies aren't wired to carry that load indefinitely. Our minds and bodies need permission, and time, to practice relaxing.

4. Though you may not think you are worthy of time and care, God disagrees. He loved you enough to send his only son to earth to die a horrible death so you could be with Him in eternity. John 3:16, 17 says it simply:

For God so loved the world that he gave his one and only Son, that whoever believes in him shall not perish but have eternal life. For God did not send his Son into the world to condemn the world, but to save the world through him.

5. You need to learn self-care so you can be emotionally healthy enough to give of yourself to your children, family, friends, coworkers, and later on, possibly a mate.

Have I convinced you yet that taking care of yourself is important? I hope so. Let's take a closer look.

Work to Free Yourself from Any Addictions You May Have

While most of the advice I describe in this chapter can be considered fun, the first one isn't fun, but painful and difficult. Ask yourself if you're addicted to any substances. Do you rely on alcohol to get you through the day? Do you look forward to your first drink? Does that first drink come earlier and earlier in the day? If so, you're not alone. Many abuse victims struggle with addictions. You've been abused, which was a harrowing experience. You may be suffering from depression and/or anxiety. Perhaps your abuser used drugs or alcohol to keep control over you. Your addiction is not something to feel guilty about, but it is something to *do something* about.

What about drugs? If you are using marijuana, or any illegal substance, you must work to free yourself from these right away. These substances are dead-end roads to despair. While you may not take illegal drugs, you may be addicted to prescription drugs or even over-the-counter medications. Be honest with yourself. Do you use these to excess? If you told your mother, best friend, or pastor the number of pills you take daily, would you be embarrassed?

Perhaps you don't struggle with these things, but you do struggle with what is known as a process addiction. Process addictions are anything you do repeatedly and to excess to make yourself feel better, such as gambling, eating, sleeping, shopping, having sex, watching television, spending time on the Internet and social media, watching any amount of pornography—even exercise can be an addiction if done to excess.

Yes, you've been through a terrible ordeal. When you were being abused, your addiction helped you cope with your pain and stress. Now you are free, and your addiction is no longer a coping mechanism; now it is a vice standing in the way of your healing. You are taking an important step toward healing by reading this book. Next, you will have to disengage yourself from your addiction(s).

This will be difficult, and you cannot do it alone. The best results come from joining a support group such as Alcoholics Anonymous, Narcotics Anonymous, Gamblers Anonymous, or Celebrate Recovery. There are many others, depending on your addiction. Be honest with yourself, and seek help immediately. *The advice I give in the rest of this book will be worthless if you are strangled by an addiction.*

Resist the Temptation to Isolate Yourself

You may want to isolate yourself from friends and family because you are depressed. Some signs of depression include[12]:

- a change in sleep habits (sleeping more or less than usual); fatigue
- a change of appetite/weight (eating more or having no desire for food)
- indecisiveness and decreased concentration
- feelings of worthlessness and guilt
- having thoughts of suicide or death
- no longer finding pleasure in things you used to enjoy
- depressed mood
- constantly feeling worked up/keyed up.

If you think you may be depressed, please read Chapter 6 about seeking counseling.

You may want to isolate yourself because you are embarrassed by your abuse, especially if you are a Christian. Domestic violence is a hard topic for many to discuss. Some people may not know what to say, and others may have strong opinions about your life decisions. You may be surprised at how little emotional support you have received from family, friends, and other church members. They may have never seen your ex-partner behave badly, and they believe you should take him back. Many Christians may believe you have "no right to divorce," and won't hesitate to let you know it. Experiencing situations like these may make you hesitate to leave the house for fear of who you might bump into, or make you afraid to open up to people because of the hurtful responses you have already received.

If you have experienced this type of thing, what should you do? I don't recommend hiding out in your home. Prepare a gentle but firm response to use the next time someone feels they have a right to comment on your decisions. You might say something like, "I am sure you have my best interest at heart, and I thank you for your concern. However, you didn't experience what I did, so you can't understand what I went through. I made the best decisions I could, based on what happened in my life. I know you will honor my right to decide what is best for me, just as I allow you to decide what is best for you." If they continue to harass you after you say this, smile and walk away. Part of the healing process is learning to make, and stand by, your decisions. You don't owe anyone an explanation.

Alternatively, you may find many who support you and your decision to leave your abuser. You will not know if you're hiding out at home. Many people today satisfy themselves with "cyber" friends, i.e., friends they find via their computer, as with Facebook, Twitter, Snapchat, and the like. While I believe these social media friends have their place, I strongly believe cyber friends do not take the place of the real flesh and blood friends we can see and touch. A hug from a friend is incredibly healing.

> Flesh and blood friends will help you more than cyber friends. Leave the house and be with real people.

What if you don't have supportive friends? I recommend you find a domestic violence support group. Contact your nearest women's crisis center and ask them to recommend one. Churches in your area may also offer them. I have experienced great healing from both. You might be surprised how similar your new friends' stories of abuse sound to yours. You will realize you are not the only person who has suffered abuse.

Another great source of healing may come from finding a mentor at your church. Many churches will match older women with younger women. I asked my church for a mentor when I was escaping my abusive ex-husband. She met with me every week for years. Even though we no longer live near each other, I still call her whenever I struggle with a problem. She helps me focus on the Lord, and I always feel better after I talk to her. Each mentor/mentee relationship will look different. You may feel comfortable sharing your past abuse, or you may not. Your mentor may or may not have experience with abuse in her past. Hopefully, she will be someone with healthy boundaries, is mature in her relationship with the Lord, and will pray for and with you.

My friend Laurie looks for people in her life she respects, and thinks of them as role models. They could be friends, coworkers, relatives, or church members. These people usually handle stress well, have a positive attitude, and display a good work ethic. Laurie learns from them as she observes and interacts with them. Doing this encourages her to associate with people she respects and admires rather than choosing friends who will tell her what she wants to hear.

You may think you don't need people, but only God, for your healing. God disagrees. Hebrews 10:24, 25 says:

And let us consider how we may spur one another on toward love and good deeds, not giving up meeting together, as some are in the habit of doing, but encouraging one another.

God gave us each other to be His hands and feet. We are each a part of Christ's body, the church, as it says in 1 Corinthians 12:14-21:

Even so the body is not made up of one part but of many.

Now if the foot should say, "Because I am not a hand, I do not belong to the body," it would not for that reason stop being part of the body. And if the ear should say, "Because I am not an eye, I do not belong to the body," it would not for that reason stop being part of the body. If the whole body were an eye, where would the sense of hearing be? If the whole body were an ear, where would the sense of smell be? But in fact God has placed the parts in the body, every one of them, just as he wanted them to be. If they were all one part, where would the body be? As it is, there are many parts, but one body.

The eye cannot say to the hand, "I don't need you!"
And the head cannot say to the feet, "I don't need you!"

No, we cannot say to one another, "I don't need you." We do need one another, just as our bodies need our hands, feet, and eyes. Spending time alone with God reading our Bibles, in private worship and prayer, is important. But it isn't enough. We need to hear our pastors preach the word to gain new insights. We need to pray for others and have them pray for us. We need to serve others and be served to fully grasp how Christ serves us. The love of God is best felt through the arms and love of His people.

Take Care of Your Physical Body

Leaving—and healing from—an abusive relationship is extremely stressful. Your body may show the signs of the stress. While dealing with your emotions may make sense to you, you may neglect your physical health, not realizing how much your physical health affects your emotional and spiritual health.

Many former abuse victims have physical ailments that have no apparent causes. I personally suffer from migraine headaches, Irritable Bowel Syndrome (IBS), and interstitial cystitis (constant pain in the bladder). Other former victims I know suffer from fibromyalgia, chronic fatigue syndrome, diabetes, asthma, and eating disorders.

Due to your many life changes, you may think you have no time to take care of your body. You may be suddenly working full time, and now you are the only parent in your kids' lives. You may be caring for a home by yourself, not to mention all the emotional strain you and your children are experiencing. However, if you neglect taking care of your physical body, you will not be able to do all the things you need to do. You should plan to:

- Spend a few minutes outdoors in natural sunlight each day. This will help you absorb vitamin D, but more importantly, it will help you fight depression. People who get no natural sunlight are more apt to become depressed.[14]

- Learn one or more relaxation techniques to help combat stress and anxiety. Spend a few minutes a day practicing a technique.

- Exercise three times a week—and you don't need to join an expensive gym. Walk up and down the stairs of your apartment or office building, take your dog for a long walk, or ride bikes with your kids.

- Eat three well-balanced meals a day; lay off the caffeine and chocolate. While they may make you feel better in the short term, they often trigger headaches. Stay away from French fries, cookies, and chips. These empty calories may taste good while you're eating them, but they do little to protect you from viruses and do not strengthen your muscles and bones; instead, they add pounds you don't need. Eat mainly lean meats, fruits, and vegetables. They have less calories and preservatives. And if you eat at home the majority of the time rather than eating out, you will save a lot of money and get more quality time with your kids.

- Get at least seven or eight hours of sleep a night; make sleep a priority. Lack of sleep will have a negative effect on your body and mind.

Try to limit the list of things that "must" be done. If you have children, enlist their help—you don't have to be super-mom.

> Taking care of your physical body is wise:
> - Get sunshine daily
> - Exercise regularly
> - Eat a healthy diet
> - Get enough sleep
> - Go to the doctor when needed

- See your medical doctor when you should. Schedule yearly checkups with your gynecologist and general/family practitioner. Make sure you get your pap smears and mammograms when you should. When you get sick, don't suffer in silence; go to the doctor and get some medicine. Nothing will halt your healing more than finding out you have cancer you could have caught earlier, or realizing a simple cold has turned to pneumonia.

Indulge Yourself Daily

Plan to do at least one kind thing for yourself each day. Make a list of simple life pleasures you enjoy. These ideas don't have to cost anything or take very much time. Examples:

- take a hot bath
- read a novel
- drink a cup of hot tea while you read a magazine
- call your sister or best friend
- exercise (more on this below).

The time you invest in yourself will have several benefits. You will find your self-esteem improving as you put yourself first, and your stress will decrease as you take these short breaks.

Regularly Practice Relaxation Techniques

Healing from emotional abuse can be painful. As you begin to address difficult memories and work toward healing, you may find yourself becoming stressed and anxious. This may even cause you physical pain at times. If you ever become afraid for yourself or others, call 911 immediately. To help relieve and/or prevent stress, you might find practicing relaxation wise. Some of these might sound "New Age," but they don't need to be. You can worship God while you learn to relax.

While you lived with your abuser, you were under continual stress. You may find your body has forgotten how to relax. These techniques can help reteach it. Use them when you feel extremely stressed, before reading a difficult chapter of this book, and before or during a counseling appointment.

Relaxation Breathing[15]

The key to deep breathing is to breathe deeply from the abdomen and get as much fresh air as possible in your lungs. When you take deep breaths from the abdomen, rather than shallow breaths from your upper chest, you inhale more oxygen. The more oxygen you get, the less tense, short of breath, and anxious you feel.

- Sit comfortably with your back straight. Put one hand on your chest and the other on your stomach.

- Breathe in through your nose. The hand on your stomach should rise. The hand on your chest should move very little.

- Exhale through your mouth, pushing out as much air as you can while contracting your abdominal muscles. The hand on your stomach should move in as you exhale, but your other hand should move very little.

- Continue to breathe in through your nose and out through your mouth. Count slowly as you exhale.

If you find it difficult breathing from your abdomen while sitting up, try lying on the floor. Put a small book on your stomach, and try to breathe so that the book rises as you inhale and falls as you exhale.

Visualization Meditation

Journal Your Journey

My counselor called this "going to your happy place." She asked me to choose a place I'd been where I was able to completely relax. Also, a place I had been alone (when you imagine yourself with others, sometimes your emotions about them get in the way of the relaxation). My counselor asked me to write as much as I could about this place as I experienced it, detailing all five senses. I chose the beach I went to every year as a child. I pictured the waves crashing on the sand, the sound of the birds calling to each other, the feel of the grains of sand and the hot sun on my back, the smell of sun lotion, and the taste of my favorite ice cream cone. Being a writer, I wrote five pages. My husband wrote about a cabin in the woods, and filled all of one paragraph. Do whatever feels right to you! The more detail you use, the easier it will be to imagine yourself actually there. I also sometimes use this to get back to sleep if I wake up in the night stressing over things I can't control.

Yoga

I put off taking a yoga class for years, though many friends had recommended it to me. I knew it is often seen as very New Age, and even considered anti-Christian, and I didn't want to deal with that. When I finally tried it, I found that to indeed be true. But when instructors begin giving New Age advice, I just pray to Jesus.

Yoga movements are helpful for relaxation. What I found most interesting, though, was when I started to cry at the beginning of my second class. I really wanted to weep, though I held back. This happened again at the end of the class. The instructor explained that we hold trauma in our bodies. He was excited his class had begun the process of releasing the emotions I had experienced more than ten years ago. He said he would welcome me weeping during his class!

Massage

I have found massage extremely helpful in dealing with my daily physical pain, and I know it is helpful for many other former abuse victims. There are many massage membership chains popping up all over the US where you can get a regular massage for a reasonable price. Massage schools also offer low-cost or free massages so their students can get practice.

If you have been sexually abused, or if you struggle with PTSD (see Chapter 6), you might find it hard at first to relax enough to enjoy a massage. If this is you, search for a massage therapist who is trained in therapeutic or medical massage. Let your therapist know about your past abuse and ask her to work with you to overcome your fears.

Other Forms of Physical Healing

Acupuncture

In the past, acupuncture was looked down upon as Eastern medicine and not considered valid by Western medical culture. This is no longer the case. Many standard medical schools now offer training in acupuncture, and it can manage the symptoms of a variety of ailments, such as migraines, asthma, chronic pain, IBS, and fibromyalgia.

Prayer

The Bible says to ask God for healing. James 5:14, 15 says:

> Is anyone among you sick? Let them call the elders
> of the church to pray over them and anoint them with oil in
> the name of the Lord. And the prayer offered in faith will
> make the sick person well; the Lord will raise them up.

Sometimes our unexplained illnesses are caused by spiritual, rather than physical, ailments. There are many examples in the Bible of people being healed through prayer (Acts 3:1-10, 19:11). Though we live in the "age of reason," we should not discount our God's ability to heal our physical bodies. He can and often does. He would do it more often if we would only ask him. See Chapter 8 for more about fighting spiritual battles with spiritual weapons.

Take Care of Your Emotions

Taking care of your emotions is just as important as taking care of your physical body.

Be Patient with Yourself and the Healing Process

Healing takes time. The longer your abuse lasted, the longer your healing will likely take. Don't set unrealistic expectations for yourself. In fact, I would recommend not setting any expectations about your healing. Allow your soul to heal on its own timetable, and allow God to work through you as He wishes. Give yourself some grace.

You may feel wonderfully strong for several days in a row, then be surprised when you wake up feeling fearful, uncertain, or depressed the next day, even wishing you were back in your abusive relationship. Or, you may feel great, and suddenly something unexpected "triggers"[15] you, and you feel you are back in the midst of the abuse. This is normal. You can expect your healing process to feel like two steps forward and one step back. You may even feel it is sometimes one step forward, two steps back! As long as you are generally moving forward, do not be alarmed.

If you find yourself sinking into a deep depression, thinking of harming yourself or others, or contemplating suicide, I recommend you get help immediately. Call 911[16] immediately. Seek counseling for less urgent needs. (I discuss this further in Chapter 6.)

> Chances are good you repeat negative comments to yourself that your abuser used to say. You can train yourself to replace those negative thoughts with positive thoughts.

Stop Negative Self-Talk

During your former relationship, did your ex verbally abuse you or say negative things about you, like you are "stupid," "don't do anything right," "you're so ugly no one will ever want you," or other derogatory things about your appearance?

If so, chances are good you have internalized his negative comments without being aware of it. We keep a running commentary in our minds all day long. Try this exercise:

Journal Your Journey

Write down everything you say to yourself over the course of a week. You may be surprised how often you say something negative to yourself. You might be repeating disparaging remarks your abuser used to say. You might also be repeating comments you heard as a child from your parents, teachers, or a bully. It's extremely important to recognize what you tell yourself regularly.

Once you have a list of negative things you say to yourself, you can begin to substitute new, positive thoughts for your old negative ones. Often negative thoughts start with "I have to . . . " or "I must . . . " or "I always/ never . . . " Be careful to frame the new thoughts in positive language instead of negative; i.e., don't use "don't." For example:

Old, Negative Thoughts	New, Positive Thoughts
I'm so stupid	I am so smart

I never do anything right	I am so capable
I'm not smart enough to understand	Look how much I am learning
I'm always picking a fight	I am a real peacemaker
I have elephant thighs	My legs are so strong
My hair looks like a rat's nest	I love my hair's natural curl
I'm so ugly; I'll never find a mate	I am desirable

Whenever you find yourself thinking one of the old, negative thoughts, purposely speak the new, positive thought instead. You will find yourself thinking the positive thoughts about yourself more and more, and the negative thoughts will fade over time.

Schedule Stressful Thoughts

Are you a worrier? I am. I often find myself consumed with unreasonable fears. I recently heard of an idea that helps. I read it in *It's My Life Now: Starting Over After an Abusive Relationship or Domestic Violence* by Meg Kennedy Dugan, M.A., and Roger R. Hock, PhD.[17] The authors call this idea thought partitioning. They base their idea on the elephant-in-the-room game. Let's say I told you not to think about the pink elephant sitting in the corner of the room. You would have trouble thinking about anything else! Thought partitioning uses the same philosophy. If I tell you not to think about the things that worry you, your worries will be at the forefront of your mind. Therefore, rather than worrying constantly, they recommend setting aside specific times to worry.

Journal Your Journey

Write down all the things you worry about for a week. Don't censor them; just write them down as they come to you. Then look over your list. Do you see patterns? Do you worry about money, your safety, or your kids? Next, schedule a "worry break" that works for you. Decide that you will work for 30 or 45 minutes (whatever you think you can sustain), then set aside 10 minutes to . . . worry. During those 10 minutes, worry as hard as you can! Then, return to work. Eventually you can move your worry breaks farther apart. If a worrisome thought intrudes during your work time, you can say, "Not now, I'll get to you later!"

Prioritize Your To-Do List

This goes along with scheduling your stressful thoughts. One of the things I stress about is having too many things to do. When you begin stressing about everything you must do, take out a sheet of paper and write down everything you need to do. For me, seeing it on paper sometimes makes it less stressful because the list isn't as long as I thought it was. Once you've written everything down, break the list into short-term, medium-term, and long-term goals. Short-term goals would be things you can *realistically* accomplish *today*. These would be tasks like calling your mother, taking a walk with your kids, washing two loads of laundry, or going to the grocery store.

Prioritize the most important items. If you have no food in the house, your most important task will probably be getting to the grocery store. If you have no clean clothes to wear, you will probably want to do some laundry. If you're feeling really stressed, don't try to do all of these things in one day; just pick one or two. When you decide on the list for today, say to yourself: "Don't panic. Do one thing at a time. Do the best you can." Repeat this as often as necessary.

Once you get the hang of setting goals for yourself and understanding how much you can accomplish in a day, you will know what you can expect from yourself. If you get to the end of a day and you still have several tasks on your list, don't fret. First decide if they really need to be done. If not, take them off the list. If so, add them to your list for tomorrow, or move them to your medium- or long-term goal list.

Long-term goals may feel overwhelming. Break these tasks into goals you can reasonably accomplish in the short and medium terms. For example, if your long-term goal is to find a job, your short-term goal for today might be to begin writing your resume. Your medium-term goal for this week could be to finish your resume, write a cover letter, and apply for one job. Your goal for next week might be to apply for three jobs.

Enjoy that feeling of accomplishment as you draw a line through a task when you complete it. One less thing to stress about!

Learn to Trust God with Your Anxiety

Scheduling your stressful thoughts and prioritizing your to-do list are great ideas. But what about those big worries that just won't go away?

You know the ones I mean, like:

- If my ex shows up at my work, will my boss fire me this time?
- Will my son turn into an abuser like his father?
- Will my daughter forgive me for not protecting her from my abuser?

The summer my divorce became final, I had the opportunity to study *Calm My Anxious Heart* by Linda Dillow.[18] The timing of the study was a perfect example of God giving me what I needed, exactly when I needed it, for I did have an anxious heart that summer. I was struggling with many *what-ifs*.

Dillow says that, for her, learning to trust God is like "playing catch" with Him. She tries to give her anxieties over to Him (by throwing Him the ball), but pretty soon, she is asking for the ball back. *Oh God, I know you have my children's best interest at heart, but do You know they are having to spend half their time with their abusive father now? . . . I know You clothe the lilies of the field, but how will I pay my bills this winter?*

Dillow says if we truly trust God, we must stop playing catch with him. We must "give Him the ball," trusting Him with the things we are worrying about, and not ask for it back.[19]

Dillow tells the story of Willis Carrier,[20] the brilliant engineer who launched the air-conditioning industry. Early in his career, Carrier was given a job he thought was impossible. He was so anxious he couldn't sleep. He devised a three-step plan to handle his anxiety:

1. Ask yourself what's the worst that can possibly happen.

2. Prepare to accept it if you have to.

3. Then calmly proceed to improve on the worst.

Carrier said that after deciding the worst that could happen—the company would lose money, and he would be fired from his job—and then reconciling himself to accepting it, he felt a sense of peace. From that time on, he was able to calmly put his energy into trying to improve on the worst *what-if.*

Linda thought this was helpful, but wasn't sure it was biblical. She searched the Bible and decided it was! The apostle Paul had faced the worst his enemies could do to him and was able to say, *"For to me, to live is Christ and to die is gain"* (Philippians 1:21). Because of this attitude, he was able to proclaim the gospel all over the world without fear.

Queen Esther is another example. She knew if she went before the king with her plea to take back his order to put all Jews to death, she might die. She said, *"If I perish, I perish"* (Esther 4:16). She faced the possibility of death, asked for prayer, then came up with a plan to try to keep the worst from happening.

Do you play catch with God? Try using Willis Carrier's three-step approach. Then, throw the ball to God and trust Him with the results.

Allow Yourself Time to Mourn

. . . to comfort all who mourn . . .
—ISAIAH 61:2

Finding you need to mourn the loss of your abusive relationship may surprise you. Even if you ended the relationship, and you are generally happy about it, you have experienced many losses that need to be mourned. Let's examine some things you may have lost.

1. **A friend and companion**: even though he was abusive at times, your partner was someone you could share your highs and lows with, talk through problems with, and work alongside (at least at times, or in the early days) to find solutions.

2. **Valued possessions**: perhaps he broke or stole items that were precious to you, or you had to give them up when you separated.

3. **Your home**: you may have had to leave your home when you left the relationship.

4. **Your job**: if you needed to move to escape your abuser, you probably lost your job.

5. **Friends and family**: you may have been close to his family and friends, and now you've lost those relationships.

6. **Your children or your dream of children**: if you wanted children but never had them, you may fear you never will. If you did have children with him, perhaps you had to leave your children behind to escape the relationship, even temporarily. Or you must now share custody with your abuser, or your relationship with your chil-

dren feels damaged because of your decision to leave. You may be mourning your dream of a healthy, "intact" family in which to raise your children.

7. **Your dreams**: perhaps you were sure he was "the one." Maybe you feel like you broke a promise to him, yourself, your friends and family, and/or God when you left the relationship.

8. **Part of yourself**: perhaps you are mourning the years you lost to the abuse and the ways you acted because of it. Maybe you feel as if you're not the same person you once were, you don't like the person you've become, and even find yourself believing you can never get that person back again. Take heart. Chances are good that the parts of yourself you feel are missing are not completely gone. They will begin to reappear as you journey toward healing. In addition, new, stronger parts of you will emerge.

You may feel one, some, or nearly all of the above losses. There may be others I haven't mentioned. The point is that you have lost some things that were valuable to you, and overcoming these losses will take time. People around you may not understand your need to mourn these losses. They may say, "You are so lucky to be rid of that abuser! Why are you crying?"

Our culture is uncomfortable with the idea of mourning. If someone appears sad, everyone tries to joke her into laughing. This is not the case, however, in every culture. In Orthodox Judaism[21], after the death of a parent, there is a ritual week of mourning when the children do not leave the house. During the first three days, mourners do not respond when spoken to. After the first three days, friends can visit, but the *friends* are the hosts; the mourners' only responsibility is to mourn. For the next three weeks, mourners slowly reenter society, but often have a tear in their clothing, and they do not shave. Full mourning does not end until an entire year after the death. During that year, entertaining and amusement is curtailed.

During the Civil War era in the southern United States[22], a widow wore black from head to toe, and a heavy veil, for one year and a day, and sometimes for as long as two and a half years. For several months, she was not to go to any social events. After her time of "deep mourning," she went into "half mourning" and was allowed to wear lavender or gray. She was not allowed to remarry for up to four years after the death of her husband.

You have not experienced a death, but you have experienced the death of a relationship and the death of a dream. Allow yourself to feel this loss. If you don't, you will never fully be healed. You must mourn your losses in order to heal from them. You may feel you will never stop feeling sad, or you may fear the extent of your sadness or rage. Crying is OK. Find someone (besides your children; they have their own grief with which to deal) who will listen to you and share your grief. This could be a friend, a support group, or a counselor. The sooner you allow yourself to feel your loss, the better off you will be later.

> Allow yourself to feel the losses you've experienced. Mourning these losses is an important part of your healing process.

Perhaps you don't believe you have anything that you need to mourn. Spend some time examining the list of losses I started this section with. Think through what your life looked like before you met your abuser, and compare it to what your life looks like now. Be honest with yourself. Are you better or worse off? What losses have you experienced?

I had trouble learning to mourn. I had become a master at denying my feelings when I lived with my abusive husband. He would ridicule me if I ever cried in front of him. He accused me of manipulating him with my tears, saying I had no reason to be sad. Also, I tried to hide my sorrow from people outside our home because he would be furious if he knew I told anyone what he was doing at home. After years of living like this, I could laugh and smile easily, but I had forgotten how to cry. Once I left the relationship, I would usually laugh when I described the worst abuse I had suffered.

If you, like me, have learned to deny your emotional pain, how can you begin to feel the pain you've denied for such a long time? Spend some time alone. Maybe you will do this in a dark room, at a coffee shop, or on a long walk, run, or drive. Whatever works best for you, do it. Think about the losses you've suffered. As you begin to feel sadness, anger, anxiety, guilt, or other negative feelings, try not to talk yourself out of them. Don't allow others to, either. Your family and friends may not like you spending time in mourning, and they may not understand why this is an important part of your journey to healing. If you don't do it now, though, your grief will never fully go away, and you will never fully heal.

Journal Your Journey

Write your feelings in a journal. Each time you allow yourself to mourn, reread what you have written, and add to those feelings. Over time, you will hopefully see your grief dissolving. If not, please read Chapter 6 of this book, and seek counseling.

Summary

Former abuse victims often find self-care challenging, but it is vital to healing from abuse. Once you begin to take care of yourself physically and emotionally, you will be better able to move forward in your journey to healing.

A Drink of Water for the Journey

"If you are traveling with a child or someone who requires assistance, secure your oxygen mask first, and then assist the other person."

—AIRLINE SAFETY SPEECH

1. Are you uncomfortable with the idea of taking care of yourself? Can you see why self-care is necessary for your healing process? Why or why not?

2. Do you tend to isolate yourself or depend on cyber friends? What are some ways you can spend more time with supportive friends?

3. Have you been taking care of your physical needs? If not, what things can you commit to begin doing today?

4. Do you find you often speak negatively to yourself? What types of things do you say? What positive statements can you replace those negative statements with?

5. Do you often feel stressed? Do the suggestions about scheduling your stressful thoughts and prioritizing your to-do list seem helpful? Why or why not?

6. Do you struggle with trusting God with your really tough anxieties? Would you be willing to try Willis Carrier's three-step method for handling your problems without worry?

7. Have you already spent time mourning your losses? Will you commit to spending more time mourning the losses you've experienced?

CHAPTER 4

Check Your Relationship with the Lord

. . . and provide for those who grieve in Zion—
to bestow on them a crown of beauty
instead of ashes . . .

—Isaiah 61:3

When you are hurting, are you apt to reach out and seek help from others, or are you more the type to "pull yourself up by your bootstraps" and try to fix yourself? If you fall into the second camp, you may find that you have subconsciously left God out of the equation of your healing. Or perhaps you are angry with God, and this makes you feel guilty.

Whether you have allowed your relationship with God to drift away, you are angry with Him, or you never really knew Him, I hope you'll be open to examining your relationship with God because I believe we need a true relationship with Him in order to fully heal from abuse.

Are You Angry with God?

If you feel distant from God, ask yourself why. If you are honest with yourself, you might find you are angry with Him and have been afraid to admit it to yourself and to Him. Perhaps you are fully aware you are angry with God; in fact, you *loathe* Him. After all, if He is all-powerful, all-loving, and all-knowing, couldn't He have prevented the abuse you've suffered? The answer is yes, He could have. But he didn't. And this makes you angry.

You are in good company. Some of the heroes of the Bible were angry with God, and the Bible gives us varying accounts of their anger and how they resolved it.

Look at the life of Job, whom God calls blameless, upright, and the Lord's servant. His ten children are killed, along with all his servants. His animals are stolen, his house is destroyed, and while he is mourning these losses, his entire body breaks out in painful sores (see Job Chapters 1 and 2). While he is reeling from all this, his "friends" arrive to tell him all this occurred because of Job's sin (Job Chapter 4)! How did Job react? He didn't pretend everything was OK. He cursed the day he was born and wrestled mightily with God.

In Chapter 31, Job lists all the ways he has tried to follow the Lord, including giving justice to his servants, helping the poor, and refusing to worship idols, look with lust at young women, or curse his enemies. Then, he exclaims:

> These heroes of the Bible were angry with God:
> - Job
> - Jacob
> - David

> *"Oh, that I had someone to hear me! I sign now my defense—let the Almighty answer me; let my accuser put his indictment in writing"*
> *(Job 31:35).*

In other words: "God, I have been righteous my entire life. Why did you allow this suffering to come to me?"

We also see King David wrestling with God in many of the Psalms (see Psalms 6, 10, 55), pouring out his despair, anger, and fear. Even Jacob wrestled with God's angel all night, refusing to let go until God blessed him, even though he experienced a dislocated hip (Genesis 32:24-32).

Have you ever honestly faced your anger toward God? If you have shared it with another Christian, you may have heard, "How can you say that about God? Shame on you! You know God is all-loving! I'm sure he had a purpose in putting you through your abuse!" Or, perhaps you have never told anyone about your feelings, but are too ashamed to give voice to them. Allowing yourself to be angry is an important part of the process of healing; it is not the joyful part of the process, but it is vital.

How Can You Heal Your Anger Toward God?

The first step in healing anger you may be feeling toward God is taking an honest inventory of your feelings. In order to do this, you might want to consider the character of God as described in the Bible. In his book *Mending the Soul, Understanding and Healing Abuse*[23] Steven R. Tracy describes seven characteristics of God. He says Satan tries to distance us from God by distorting these characteristics, so it is important for abuse survivors to understand who God really is.

1. **Loving**: God is loving, compassionate, and shows mercy toward those who suffer (Exodus 3:7, Matthew 9:36, Romans 5:8). Perhaps you believe God loves other people but not you. Or maybe you believe you must earn God's love, and if you are not always good He will no longer love you, or maybe you believe God doesn't care about the suffering you've experienced. The truth is God loves all believers unconditionally and eternally. He doesn't love them because they are good; they are accepted because *He* is good. God is deeply grieved by your suffering.

2. **Wise** (Omniscient): God knows everything that ever happened, is happening now, and will happen in the future (1 Samuel 16:7, Jeremiah 1:5, Ephesians 3:9-11). You may believe you can't be honest with God, that He will be disgusted with you because He knows all your secret sins, or that because no one believes what happened to you, the truth will never come out. The truth is God loves you in spite of knowing everything about you. No abuse is ever hidden from God, nor does it escape His justice.

> God's Characteristics:
> 1. Loving
> 2. Wise (Omniscient)
> 3. All-Powerful (Sovereign, Omnipotent)
> 4. Holy, Pure
> 5. Righteous, Just
> 6. Faithful
> 7. Eternal

3. **All-Powerful** (Sovereign, Omnipotent): He has absolute rule over all creation and He is good (Genesis 50:20, Psalm 103:19, Jeremiah 29:11). You may believe God is a cruel king who cannot be trusted, that He isn't good because He didn't prevent your abuse, and that He waits to further hurt you. The truth is God can and eventually will bring good out of evil, and you can trust Him with your life. He is bigger than your abuser, and He will ultimately triumph over all evil.

4. **Holy, Pure**: God is distinct and separate from the world He created. He is morally pure and He never sins (Isaiah 6:1-7, Revelation 4:8). You may believe God is too pure to love someone like you, someone who has done so many sinful things in her life. You may think He is like the Christians who have looked down on you in the past. The truth is God is different from and greater than anyone on earth. He sent His own Son to die for your sins, and now He doesn't remember them (Isaiah 43:25, Psalm 103:12).

5. **Righteous, Just**: God is morally perfect; He always does what is right because of His perfect character (Psalm 58:10, 11; Hebrews 10:1-18; Revelation 16:4-6). You may believe there is no justice in the universe because your abuser wasn't punished as fully as you would have liked. You may fear God will eventually punish you, and that you deserve to burn in hell. The truth is, no one can ever condemn God's children because Christ's perfect sacrifice satisfied the justice of God. God is a just judge; He will never allow unrepentant evil to go unpunished.

6. **Faithful**: God is absolutely loyal and dependable. He fulfills one hundred percent of his promises (Psalm 25:10; 1 Thessalonians 5:2; 2 Thessalonians 3:2, 3). You may believe no one and nothing can be trusted, not even God, and not the Bible. You may think God will eventually lose patience with you as have other people in your life. The truth is God always does what He says He will, and you can trust His promises. No matter how many people abuse and betray you, God will never give up on you.

Read the seven characteristics of God. Then, using your journal:

1. Ask God to reveal His true character to you.
2. Tell Him your true feelings.
3. Ask Him hard questions.
4. Listen for His response.

7. **Eternal**: God is free from all constraints of time. He sees everything—past, present, and future—with perfect clarity. He has no beginning or end (Psalm 90:2, Isaiah 46:10, 2 Peter 3:8). You may believe you have no reason to hope in the future. You couldn't have predicted the abuse you've suffered, you can't deal with it, and you will never heal from it. You couldn't trust God in the past, and you can't trust Him for your fu-

ture. But you must instead tell yourself the truth, and that is that God was not surprised by any trial you have experienced. He has a perfect plan for your healing. You can trust him because God will fulfill His promises according to His timetable, not yours.

Journal Your Journey

Spend some time reading and praying through these characteristics of God. Be honest about the lies Satan has led you to believe because of the abuse you've experienced. Use your journal to ask God to reveal His true character to you. Tell Him your true feelings about the pain you've had. Ask Him the hard questions. He may not answer them in the way you would like. You probably will not ever get to see God face-to-face as Jacob did, or hear him audibly as Job did (although you might), but you may slowly begin to feel closer to Him as you wrestle with Him in this way.

Where Was God When You Were Being Abused?

Possibly some of the hardest questions you may face as you grow closer to God are: "Why did you allow me (and my children) to be abused?" and "Where were you when this was happening to me?" And, quite possibly, this one: "Why didn't you prevent it?" How does the Bible answer these wrenching questions? Surprisingly, the Bible *doesn't* answer them. In his book *The Question That Never Goes Away: What Is God Up to in a World of Such Tragedy and Pain?* Philip Yancey points out that when Job challenges God with the *why?* question, God actually answers him audibly. Yet, He doesn't really give him an answer. Instead, in Job Chapters 38–41, God demonstrates His strength and wisdom, and shows Job Himself.[24]

Yancey gives three answers to his own question, "What is God up to in a world of such tragedy and pain?"

Answer #1: God is on the side of those who suffer.[25]

He didn't leave us alone in our suffering. Instead, He sent His Son to earth to redeem it.

Jesus didn't come to earth with a great display of power, but came instead as a vulnerable child. During His life, Jesus saw all kinds of suffering, but He didn't give theories about why suffering exists. Instead, He forgave sin, healed the hurting, cast out evil, and even overcame death.

Yancey writes: "For whatever reason, God has chosen to let history take its course."[26] He doesn't wave a magic wand; He absorbs suffering in the person of His son, Jesus. Words don't help during suffering; we need a suffering God. Jesus' crucifixion was the worst crime in history. So why do we call it Good Friday? Jesus said He could have called on legions of angels to prevent the crucifixion, but He didn't. God's redemption of suffering goes *through* pain, not *around* it.

> Where is God when we are in pain?
>
> 1. He's on the side of the sufferer—through Jesus.
> 2. He's in the church.
> 3. He's preparing a place for us in Heaven.

Romans 8:28 teaches us about God redeeming suffering:

And we know that in all things God works for the good of those who love him, who have been called according to his purpose.

This verse can seem horribly insensitive when you are in anguish. Yancey doesn't believe (as some do) that God sends us suffering to build our character. Instead, He redeems (recycles) the suffering we encounter in the evil world we live in. For example, when I send my used pop cans to the recycling center, I am hoping they will make something useful out of my trash. In a similar way, I am hoping God will make something useful out of the "trash" of the abuse I've suffered.

When we are in anguish, we can't see how God could make anything good out of our tragedy. How will God recycle the abuse you have experienced? Many people attest that they felt closest to God when they were suffering the most. I remember feeling very close to God when I was terrified of my first husband. He was my only consolation at a time when my life seemed so dark.

Answer #2: "Where is God when we hurt?" He is in the church, God's delegated presence on earth.

God designed His church to be a place of hope on earth. Unfortunately for many abused women, too often the church does not relieve suffering, but only makes it worse. I experienced this when leaving my first husband. However, if the church does its job correctly, it can be a real arm of healing. Many churches have abuse survivor support groups and food pantries; others sponsor women's crisis centers and homeless shelters for women and children. If you are a member of a thriving, loving church community, you will have the opportunity to feel God's love surrounding you through the arms of His people.

If you have experienced pain or confusion after looking for support from your church, I am so sorry. I know how sad this is. This is not the way God designed the church to work. Churches are made up of people, which means they are full of sinners. Though one or more individual church bodies may have hurt you, I hope you won't give up on God's global church. At the end of this Chapter, I recommend you look for genuine Christian community, which can be extremely healing. In Chapter 11 of this book, I describe how God was able to redeem the pain my church caused me, and recycle it for my good and for the good of others. I pray my story can give you hope.

Answer #3: "What is God up to?" He is in Heaven, preparing a better place for us.

On the night He was betrayed, Jesus told His disciples that He was going to prepare a place for them (John 14:2). He didn't describe it in detail, but if you take a look at the book of Revelation, you can see we will live together with Jesus, and we will worship Him forever in a place too beautiful to describe. God Himself will wipe away our tears, there will be no more death or mourning or crying or pain, and He will make everything new (Revelation 21:1-5). On days when I feel fearful, sad, lonely, or angry, I try to imagine how wonderful it will be to live there with Jesus. I try to remember that my years on earth will be brief in comparison to the amount of time I will live there. Imagining eternity is hard for me. To put it in perspective, I picture a ruler laying on the beach in California.[27] I picture my life here on earth as one inch of that ruler. Then I picture my time in eternity with Jesus as the rest of the continental United States, all the way to the Atlantic Ocean. How wonderful and infinite that will be! Praise You, Lord!

Feeling Ashamed?

> *Instead of your shame*
> *you will receive a double portion,*
> *and instead of disgrace*

you will rejoice in your inheritance.
And so you will inherit a double portion in your land,
and everlasting joy will be yours.

—ISAIAH 61:7

Abusers are adept at blaming their victims for their behavior. Because of this many victims believe *his* behavior is *her* fault. This makes them feel shame for something they did not cause. In his book *Mending the Soul*, Tracy defines shame as "a deep, painful sense of inadequacy and personal failure based on the inability to live up to a standard of conduct—one's own or one imposed by others."[28] He says God gave us the ability to feel healthy shame as a correct response when we violate one of God's laws. This is a gift from God because it tells us when we are doing something wrong, and it lets us know we are moving away from our loving, holy Creator. It is a gracious call to repentance.

> Abusers are adept at making their victims believe the abuser's behavior is the *victim's* fault.

On the other hand, unhealthy, or toxic, shame can never redeem; it can only destroy. Toxic shame distorts our sin, our worth, and God's grace so that we can do nothing but hide in the shadows. It gives a false interpretation of our sin that strips us of hope.[29] Tracy points out that shame is not a reliable emotion. The Bible makes it clear that humans do not always feel shame when they are guilty, and they are tempted to feel shame when they are not guilty.[30]

In his book, Tracy gives an interesting reason why an abuse victim often takes the blame of the abuse for the abuser. He says if the victim believes it is her behavior that is causing the abuse, this enables her to preserve a sense of meaning, hope, and power. If she is bad, her abuser is good. If she tries to be good, perhaps she can stop his abuse by changing *her* behavior.[31] This allows her to have false hope that the abuse will eventually go away—if she can only be good enough.

How Can You Heal Your Shame?

Journal Your Journey

Tracy recommends writing a shame history.[32] Prayerfully construct a detailed personal history of the times in your life when you have felt the greatest shame, listing whatever created the shame. Then try to answer three questions about each event:

- *Who is responsible for this shameful event? In other words, who "owns" the blame?*
- *What do you need to confess?*
- *What do you need to make right (make restitution for)?*

You may feel ashamed about an event that was not your fault. However, you may need to confess to God actions you took afterward, such as taking drugs or alcohol to numb the pain, or abusing others. Confessing your sin to God doesn't maintain your salvation; it strengthens your walk with Him.

The final step is to make restitution for anything you were responsible for. This will look different depending on the circumstances. If you have emotionally damaged someone who is still in your life, you can write a note of apology, acknowledging what you've done, and offer to pay for their counseling. If the person is dead, or out of your life, you can write a symbolic letter to them. You will never give it to them, but you may be surprised how good writing the letter will make you feel. As a person recently coming out of abuse, you might find it difficult to discern the things you are responsible for and what things your abuser should own. If so, seek the help of a counselor, mentor, or friend during this step.

> In Christ we are completely forgiven, and He no longer remembers our sins.

Accept God's Judgment of Yourself

Once you understand what things you are responsible to own, and which things your abuser should own, you can begin to get rid of this toxic shame by letting God, instead of your abuser, or even yourself, define your worth. What does God say about His children?

- We are completely forgiven (Psalm 103:12).
- Nothing can separate us from His love (Romans 8:38, 39).
- He rejoices over you with singing (Zephaniah 3:17).
- He doesn't remember our sins (Isaiah 43:25).
- There is no condemnation for those who are in Christ (Romans 8:1).

Look up these verses and others that describe our relationship to the Father and prayerfully meditate on them. Accept them as truth. After all, God's Word is truth. Exchange Satan and your abuser's lies for God's truth.

Prayerfully Hand Shame Back to Your Abuser

Steven Tracy says one of the most empowering things you can do to get rid of shame that belongs to your abuser is to symbolically hand the shame back to him.[33] In many Psalms[34], the authors ask God to shame their abusive enemies. This had two purposes:

- to cause the abuser to be overwhelmed with shame for his or her sin so they would repent, and

- to bring utter destruction to the abuser if he or she didn't repent.

Does this sound un-Christian to you? God is a God of justice. He knows we long for justice when we have been abused. In Romans 12:19, He tells us not to take revenge on our enemies, but to allow *Him* to avenge us. He knows we don't have the power and authority to properly exact justice on abusers. His justice, however, will be perfect and inescapable. We may not see it in our lifetime, although we might. He will exact most of his justice in the afterlife. If we pray our abuser will be filled with shame, he may repent. If he does, his life will be completely changed. He will be ashamed of his treatment of you. He will stop behaving abusively to you or anyone else. He will try to make restitution to you and others he has hurt. If he does not repent, he will receive everlasting punishment.

> To hand shame to your abusers, ask God to overwhelm them with shame for their sins so they will repent, or that He will bring them to destruction if they won't.

Choose to Reject Shame

We live in a world full of sin. Because of this, we won't be able to stop people from trying to shame us, but we can refuse to accept the shame they try to hand us from this moment forward. Jesus is our perfect example of this. He died the most shameful death known to man, crucifixion. People he loved abandoned him, betrayed him, or were embarrassed by him. The crowds that had lauded him a week earlier now jeered at him and stared at his embarrassment. However, Hebrews 12:2 says:

For the joy set before him he endured the cross, scorning its shame, and sat down at the right hand of the throne of God.

While hanging practically naked on the cross, Jesus prayed:

"Father, forgive them, for they do not know what they are doing."

—LUKE 23:34

Shedding the shame of others, especially from your abuser or other family members, may be difficult for you, because you might be used to accepting other people's judgment of you. If they treat you shamefully, you must deserve it, right? *Wrong!*

Journal Your Journey

How can you begin to shed the shame messages others send your way (or you find yourself thinking), either those actually spoken out loud or implied by their behavior? Tracy recommends writing down each shame message you receive, and then look for what is false about each statement, based on biblical truth. You might want to memorize Bible verses that refute the lies others tell you about yourself. For example, if someone says you are ugly, you can memorize Psalm 139:14:

I praise you because I am fearfully and wonderfully made;
your works are wonderful,
I know that full well.

If someone says God won't forgive you for leaving your abusive husband, you can memorize Romans 8:1:

Therefore, there is now no condemnation for those who are in Christ Jesus.

Experience Genuine Christian Community

Finally, finding a group of Christians you can be real with will help you heal from shame. This might be a support group, life group, Bible study group, or adult Sunday school class. The format of the group doesn't matter as long as each member feels safe to let others see who they really are. In the group, hopefully, you will confess your sins to each other (James 5:16), be emotionally honest about your joys and sorrows (Romans 12:15), give and receive love (Romans 16:16), meet each other's needs (Acts 2:45, Galatians 6:2), pray for each other (James 5:16), challenge each other (1 Thessalonians 5:14), and help each other if you fall into sin (Galatians 6:1).

> Being around healthy Christians will begin to heal your relationship with God, others, and yourself.

You may need to search to find a group like this, but you will be blessed by it, and it will help you overcome your shame. It will begin to heal your relationship with God, others, and yourself. I personally recommend Community Bible Study (CBS), of which I was a member for many years. This is a structured Bible study with a lot of great fellowship built in. I recommend you try it if there is a class near you. (Go to www.communitybiblestudy.org to learn more.) If you can't find a CBS class near you, look for a Bible study at your church or a church nearby.

What If You Just Don't Know God Very Well?

Perhaps you consider yourself a Christian, but you have no real relationship with Jesus. You may be surprised I would even talk about having a relationship with Him. Jesus is fully God and fully human. He wants to know you intimately, like a close friend. The only way we can know a person is to spend time with him. The best way I know to spend time with Jesus is to read the book He ordained to be written, the Bible. I recommend you begin by reading the gospels, the first four books of the New Testament: Matthew, Mark, Luke, and John. In these books you will get to know Jesus. You will see Him loving tortured women (John 8:1-11), healing the sick (Luke 8:40-47), and dying for the sins of the world (Luke 23).

> If you are just beginning to read the Bible, read the gospels or the Psalms.

I also recommend you read the Psalms. In them, David and other psalmists poured out their hearts to God when they were treated abusively. I was constantly amazed by how close their prayers were to mine. You can find some Psalms that speak to your situation and pray them out loud to God! I suggest Psalms 10, 17, 25, 37, 42, and 55 as an initial list.

Summary

God is the great healer. He loves you and wants to see you healed from the abuse you've suffered. Though you may at times doubt it, abuse makes Him sad and angry, and He wants to bring your abusers to justice. He also wants to have a close relationship with you. As you draw closer to God and to other healthy, loving Christians, He will work with you to heal you from your abuse.

A Drink of Water for the Journey

"God wants to restore dignity, virtue, and honor to women in a world that demoralizes them."

—BETH MOORE IN BREAKING FREE[35]

1. Are you angry with God? If so, explain why.

2. Do you have trouble believing God is loving, wise, all-powerful, holy, righteous, faithful, and eternal?

3. Has the church been a comfort to you, or has it caused you more pain? Explain. If it has caused you more pain, are you willing to try to find a loving church, Bible study, or support group to aid in your healing?

4. Do you suffer with feelings of shame? Where does this shame come from?

5. Write a shame history for any shameful events you struggle with.

6. Make a list of those who have abused you to pray over. Ask God to overwhelm them with shame so they can repent and thus avoid destruction.

7. Do you know God well? If not, are you willing to spend time to get to know Him better by reading His Word, doing a Bible study, or going to church?

8. If you find yourself stuck in your anger with God, or disinterested in healing your relationship with Him or His church right now, that's OK. Give yourself grace. Perhaps as you read further, your heart will change—and perhaps not. God is a gentleman; He never pushes Himself on us. He wants us to come to Him in our own time and of our own free will.

CHAPTER 5

Examine Your Past

They will rebuild the ancient ruins
and restore the places long devastated;
they will renew the ruined cities
that have been devastated for generations.

—Isaiah 61:4

Perhaps you struggle with healing from the abuse you have experienced as an adult because you were also abused as a child. If so, you are not alone. According to UNICEF, "The single best predictor of children becoming either perpetrators or victims of domestic violence later in life is whether or not they grow up in a home where there is domestic violence."[36] Children who grow up in homes where domestic violence exists are called children of domestic violence. I am one of those.

My mom married my stepfather when I was five. He was not often physically abusive, but he was verbally abusive. I grew to fear him.

Growing up as a child of domestic violence sets you up to believe things about yourself and the world that aren't true. As a small child, you looked to your parents for love, warmth, and acceptance. If you didn't receive those things, your brain wasn't mature enough to realize there was a problem with the adults in your life. Instead, you probably assumed the problem was within you. This is true of most children of domestic violence.

> Growing up as a child of domestic violence sets you up to believe things about yourself and the world that aren't true.

Children's brains are easily molded by what they see and experience. In most cases, if they are treated with hatred, they begin to believe they aren't worthy of love. If they are told they are stupid, they believe it. If they are neglected, they assume this is because there is something lacking within themselves. If they see their mother disrespected and shamed, they will believe women do not deserve to be respected, that there is something shameful about being female.

These are all lies. Satan is the father of lies, but God is truth. He wants you to be set free. In John 8:32, Jesus says,

"Then you will know the truth, and the truth will set you free."

In his book *Invincible: The 10 Lies You Learn Growing Up with Domestic Violence, and the Truths that Set You Free*, Brian Martin, founder of the Childhood Domestic Violence Association, describes the lies you may have learned as a child growing up in a home filled with domestic violence. He then provides the truths to help set you free.

The most damaging lie we learn as children of domestic violence is that we are unlovable. According to Martin, "When babies are born, they require the love and attention of their parents to survive and thrive. When we are born, we need to be touched. A newborn clings to her mother, and the powerful hormone oxytocin creates a profound bond between them. This 'cuddle chemical' is essential for milk production, nursing, and the mother's ability to bond with her baby.

> The most damaging lie children of domestic violence learn is that they are unlovable.

It triggers a feeling of strong connection. In this blissful state a child basks in the comfort of a mother's arms knowing the world is a safe place to be.

"But if when we are born, we are routinely deprived of touch and affection, the consequences are severe, the possible result being the so-called failure to thrive syndrome. This occurs when a baby is ignored, perfunctorily fed, or left alone. A child will despair and become unresponsive. In extreme cases, the baby may even stop eating, waste away, and die. That's how essential it is for humans to be consistently shown that they are loved. In the same way that infants may fail to thrive when they don't experience the physical signs of love, when children grow up living with domestic violence, they learn to question how loved they are."[37]

If you grew up believing you were unlovable, this belief—perhaps even an unconscious one—may have profoundly affected the decisions you've made as an adult, especially when it comes to choosing an intimate partner. Most abusers are incredibly charming when they begin a relationship. They may shower you with affection, compliments, and gifts. You may feel deeply in love with this person. All that powerful attention might influence anyone, but especially someone who secretly believes they aren't worthy of love.

As your relationship matured, and your abuser began to show his true character, some of the other lies you could have learned as a child of domestic violence may have worked together to keep you in the relationship. The lie that has affected me most as an adult is that I am worthless. I don't walk around consciously thinking I'm worthless. On the surface, I have pretty good self-esteem. I am able to write books, help other abuse survivors, be a good mother, friend, Christian, and more. However, when something goes wrong, like when one of my stepchildren chooses not to speak to me for no reason, I instinctively revert back to the feeling of being worthless, or "not good enough," a self-belief my stepfather taught me.

What about you? Perhaps you struggle with feeling self-conscious. Did your parents, siblings, or someone else in your childhood call you stupid, ugly, fat, worthless, or bad? The old saying, "Sticks and stones may break my bones, but words will never hurt me," is fundamentally untrue. Insults hurled at a young child can scar her and her image of herself forever. After all, if the people who are supposed to love you and protect you think you are ugly, you must be ugly, right? *Wrong!* My counselor-second husband often says, "Hurt people hurt people." Your parents, who were caught up in their personal daily hell, may have often said things that weren't true. But, as an impressionable child, it may have been easy for you to take their put-downs to heart. Now, as an adult, it may be difficult for you to change your negative opinion about yourself.

> The old saying, "Sticks and stones may break my bones, but words will never hurt me," is fundamentally untrue.

Maybe you don't struggle with feeling self-conscious, but you do struggle with feelings of fearfulness. As a child of domestic violence you had to live with fear, and this may still affect your view of the world. As a child, your world was not a safe place. As psychiatrist Sonja Lyubomirsky explains, "In a home full of pain, quarreling, or coldness, children are chronically stressed and on guard."[38] Perhaps now, as an adult, you hide, preferring to stay in the shadows or blend into the crowd. Maybe you walk around with hunched shoulders in an unconscious attempt to withdraw into yourself, seeking a sense of security you never knew when you were young. Personally, I have lots of nervous habits, like biting my knuckles, pulling my ear, and laughing at the end of sentences.

How could feeling worthless, self-conscious, or fearful have affected you once your abuser moved from the honeymoon stage of the relationship and began his abusive behaviors? If you felt worthless, you may have (subconsciously) thought you deserved to be treated with disrespect; after all, your parents treated you (or each other) that way when you were a child. If you are self-conscious, you may not have been surprised when your abuser began calling you names, as your parents or other loved ones did when you were young. And when he began treating you so abusively you began to fear him, that fear may have seemed familiar in a way. Also, as time went on, your very real fear of him may have made it harder and harder to stand up to his abuse and to think of getting away from him.

Lies Childhood Domestic Violence Teaches

According to Martin's book, *Invincible*, growing up as a child of domestic violence may have taught you many lies about yourself. Ask yourself if you believe any of the following lies:

1. **Guilty**: You should have stopped the violence; it was your fault. You now have a deep feeling of shame.

2. **Resentful**: You are guilty of not stopping the violence, so something is wrong with you. You have no compassion for yourself, so why should you have compassion for others? If you have no compassion for others, how can you be a good person?

3. **Sad**: Feeling sad is a constant that will always be with you. Even when things seem to be going well, sadness is right around the corner. This is just how you are. Because of this, you go through life

focused on yourself, consciously or subconsciously mourning the loss of your childhood.

4. **Alone**: When they are young, children of domestic violence are often unpopular because they haven't been taught how to get along with others or because they have a very low self-esteem. As an adult, you may have a hard time trusting people or making close friendships. Even when you are in a large crowd, you may feel isolated from others.

5. **Angry**: As a child, you saw the adults in your life reacting in anger, and you learned this was how to resolve conflict. When someone hurts you, or makes you feel not good enough, you can make yourself feel more powerful and in control by expressing your anger. You believe anger is an effective way to solve problems and deal with conflict.

6. **Hopeless**: You were unable to control your circumstances as a child, so you naturally began to think having a good future was hopeless. Your life was reduced to simply existing from day to day.

7. **Worthless**: If you weren't important enough for your parents to value you and keep you safe, how will anyone else value you? You need the constant approval of others to replace your lack of self-esteem. When you don't get it, you feel worth even less.

> Growing up as a child of domestic violence may have taught you to feel:
>
> • Guilty
> • Resentful
> • Sad
> • Alone
> • Angry
> • Hopeless
> • Worthless
> • Fearful
> • Self-conscious
> • Unloved

8. **Fearful**: The constant stress of your abusive childhood affects the amygdala, the part of the brain that detects danger, putting it on permanent alert. As a result, fear becomes your default response to everything, such as a siren, a dog's bark, or the phone ringing.

9. **Self-conscious**: Because of the lies you were told about your appearance or personhood as a child, you feel unattractive and flawed, as if everyone is judging you. You look to the affirmations of others to feel attractive and "good enough."

10. **Unloved**: Your parents, who were supposed to love you, didn't, so no one else will either. You aren't worthy of being loved. You don't even know what the word really means, or how it feels to really be loved. You don't think you deserve to be loved.

Truths That Set You Free

These lies keep you in bondage to your past, a place Satan loves you to be. But God wants you to know the truth and be free. What is the truth?

1. **The abuse was not your fault.** Children are never at fault for the abuse they suffer at the hands of the adults in their lives. No matter how "naughty" a child behaves, she can never cause a parent to abuse her. Parents are responsible for their own actions. You wouldn't blame your child(ren) for the abuse your partner gave you, would you?

   This lie is especially ugly for former victims of childhood sexual abuse. Often perpetrators will tell the child she somehow enticed the adult into a sexual relationship. This is *blatantly untrue*. No child can ever entice an adult or older child into a sexual relationship. The blame for that rests on the perpetrator, *not* the victim.

   > Children feel all the emotions abuse causes adults to feel, but they don't have the rational part of the brain to grasp the truth.

   Children feel all the emotions abuse causes adults to feel, but they don't have a developed, rational part of the brain to understand what is happening, to understand the truth. Now that you are an adult, you can begin to look at your childhood abuse in a more rational manner.

2. **You are loved.** Even if you have never experienced real love from a person, you are loved more than you can possibly imagine by God in Heaven (John 15:13).

3. **You are not alone.** You may feel as if you have to face the world alone, but that isn't true. Though you may not feel him, God is always by your side, and he always wants the best for you. In addition, there are many people in the world who are available to help you. You may not see them, or have ever met them, but they are there

to help. Check out my Get Help[39] page for domestic violence ho-tlines around the world. Through these, you can inquire about crisis centers, which can recommend support groups and counselors who will work at a reasonable rate.

4. **You are worthy.** Every person ever born was created in the im-age of the all-loving, all-knowing, all-powerful God (Genesis 1:27). Because of this, you have infinite worth (Matthew 6:26). You may feel as if you are too damaged, have done too many bad things, or have had too many bad things done to you to ever be worth any-thing. This is not true. The truth is, none of us has a perfect past. Romans 3:23 says: *For all have sinned, and fall short of the glory of God.* When we believe in Jesus, God gives us Jesus' righteousness. From that moment on, God doesn't look at our past, and our failures; all He sees when He looks at us is the sinless life Jesus led in our place.

> Every person ever born was created in the image of God.

5. **You can have hope for a better future.** You may feel hopeless be-cause of your past. However, God is the God of second and third chances. He will walk beside you as you struggle. Yes, many things look difficult. You experienced things a child should never have to feel. This is why we need a savior. We can't make the changes we need to make in our own power. We need someone infinitely better than we are, or than our parents were, to come alongside us, to give us His perfection. Thank God, we have a savior like that: Jesus.

Will You Be Able to Be Fully Healed?

No one can completely cure the scars of childhood trauma. We can only work through them, process them, and learn how to deal with them differently so we can feel better. In her book *Will I Ever Be Good Enough? Healing the Daughters of Narcissistic Mothers*, Dr. Karyl McBride likens our lives to a tree.[40] Each of us, like a tree, has roots (our family of origin and generational legacy); long, sturdy trunks (how we were treated as children); and branches that flower and grow in our adult lives. Your trunk bears scars, which don't really go away; they are part of who you are. But the healing work you do helps you treat any gashes, fill them in, supply balm and seal them gently, and takes away the old recurring pain, changing the original trauma and allowing you to grow around it and away from it.

Knowing you can't completely cure the scars from your childhood can actually keep you from becoming discouraged. Maybe you will be relieved to know you don't have to totally remove those scars. Your past scars are important to acknowledge; they make up who you are today. Yet, they don't define you. You can accept your past as part of who you are and move on to a brighter future.

How Can You Begin to Heal Your Soul from Your Childhood Abuse?

In his book I referenced earlier, *Mending the Soul*, Steven Tracy outlines a path toward healing childhood abuse. Tracy contends you cannot heal your past abuse until you are honest about it and truly feel the *emotions* of it.[41] He notes that many childhood victims of domestic abuse, especially of sexual abuse, instinctively minimize and take the blame for the abuse they experienced. He says you will often hear adult survivors make statements such as, "My father didn't really molest me; he just touched me inappropriately a few times." Or, "Overall, my parents really took pretty good care of me." Or, "My home wasn't really as bad as others" or "No wonder my parents got so angry with me; I was a hard child to raise."[42] Tracy says the reason we do this is to protect ourselves from acknowledging our parents didn't love us as they should have.

> Many childhood victims of abuse minimize the painful treatment to protect themselves from acknowledging their parents didn't love them as they should have.

When we minimize the abuse we've experienced, we stay in denial and deaden our emotions to our past abuse. Have you ever described an abusive event you've experienced in the same way you would give a weather report, i.e., with little to no emotion? When I first left my abusive husband, I laughed when I described his abuse of me, which made my friends very uncomfortable. This type of denial of our emotions keeps us in bondage to the trauma and prevents us from healing.

Eleanor D. Payson, M.S.W., agrees. In her book *The Wizard of Oz and Other Narcissists: Coping with One-Way Relationships in Work, Love, and Family*, Payson opines that our early traumas and unmet needs in childhood are not the most significant wounds we take with us into adulthood. She says the greater wound is our lack of opportunity or support to process our feelings about those traumatic events.[43] She says when a child experiences trauma, and is helped by a parental figure to talk about her feelings, she will be able to move forward with her "self" intact. However, if she must pretend the trauma didn't happen, or pretend she is not upset by it, and if she doesn't get to talk about her true feelings, she will carry an unhealed scar into adulthood.

> Our greatest childhood wound is not the initial trauma, but being unable to talk about and process it.

Here are the steps Mr. Tracy outlines to heal from childhood abuse.[44]

Step 1: Establish safety: Make sure you are no longer being abused before you begin this work. Check out Chapter 2, where I describe creating boundaries with your abuser. You may want to begin this work within the safety of a counselor's office (see Chapter 6) or with a trusted friend.

Step 2: Choose to face the truth and feel: You won't be able to immediately feel the emotions you may have spent many years trying to hide from and deny. However, you will have to decide you are willing to face what really happened to you and allow yourself to feel the emotions that surface.

Journal Your Journey

Step 3: Tell—and feel—the story by writing your personal trauma narrative: Write a timeline of abusive events that happened to you, at what age, and by whom. You may want to enlist the help of supportive friends and family members who were there in your childhood to fill in events and dates you have forgotten, especially if your abuse occurred when you were very young, or if you have blocked much of it from your memory. Add the responses of family members and other caregivers. Often family members contribute to your trauma by their reactions. Did they blame you? Did they insist you cover up the abuse? Did they deny it happened?

You may find this step especially challenging. Often, families intimidate abuse victims to keep secrets, and you may feel disloyal recounting your past abuse. Christians often believe people should "put the past behind them, and look toward the future." However, you cannot put the past behind you until you have looked at the truth of it and resolved the trauma.

Take a look at the story of Joseph in Genesis 37:1-36 and 42:1-50:21. Joseph's brothers were jealous of him, captured him, and sold him as a slave. Many years later, Joseph became a powerful man in Egypt. His brothers went to Egypt to beg for food because there was a famine in their land. Ironically, Joseph was the man they had to ask for their food! Joseph recognized them, but they did not recognize Joseph. Before Joseph reconciled with his brothers, he put them through many trials to help them realize the sin they had committed toward him, which caused Joseph, as well as his brothers, emotional pain. When they finally repented of their sin, Joseph revealed his identity to his brothers, and they were able to reconcile.

Joseph could have reconciled with his brothers right away, denying the pain they caused him. Instead, he chose to be honest about their abuse, causing both his brothers and him to feel the pain of their actions. Only then could a true reconciliation occur.

Step 4: Identify the distortions and reclaim God's original design: Look back at the beginning of this chapter to the list of lies domestic violence teaches children about themselves. Think about which ones you have believed about yourself. Next, think about lies you have believed about God, such as, "I can't trust Him," "He doesn't love me," "God is disgusted with me," "God is punishing me." Finally, identify the lies you have believed about others. These could include, "If others really knew me, they would reject me," "You can't trust anyone; people will only hurt you," "Men are all alike; all they want to do is use women," "No decent man will ever want me."[45]

Step 5: Repent of deadness and denial: When you were a child, you found ways to cope with the abuse you suffered. This was a good and creative ability, and helped you survive. For example, if at age nine you looked at a spot on the wall to help you tune out your abuse, you should be congratulated for that. However, if as an adult in a non-abusive re-

> When we try to shield ourselves from pain, we actually shield ourselves from life, joy, and intimacy with God and others.

lationship you protect yourself by tuning out, stiffening, or fleeing intimacy, this is no longer protecting you. Instead, you are hurting those around you, isolating yourself, and not trusting God. When we try to shield ourselves from pain, we end up shielding ourselves from life, joy, and intimacy with God and others.

Step 6: Mourn the loss and dare to hope: At the end of Chapter 3, I describe what it means to mourn. You may think I focus too much on mourning your losses. However, I believe mourning is biblical and necessary for healing. In Matthew 5:4, Jesus says,

> *Blessed are those who mourn,*
> *for they will be comforted.*

The Bible dedicates the entire book of Lamentations to mourning. When you have fully mourned, you can begin to hope, as Jeremiah did in Lamentations 3:22, 23:

> *Because of the Lord's great love we are not consumed,*
> *for his compassions never fail.*
> *They are new every morning;*
> *great is your faithfulness.*

As you truthfully face the pain your childhood abuse has caused you, both when it happened, and throughout your life, you can begin to see God face to face.

Growing Up with a Narcissistic Parent

Perhaps your childhood wasn't marked by overt abuse, whether emotional, sexual, or physical, but maybe you were raised by one or more parents who put themselves and their needs before yours. The *Diagnostic and Statistical Manual of Mental Disorders* (DSM-5),[46] published by the American Psychiatric Association, gives the following criteria for someone with narcissistic personality disorder:

- having an exaggerated sense of self-importance

- expecting to be recognized as superior even without achievements that warrant it

- exaggerating achievements and talents

- being preoccupied with fantasies about success, power, brilliance, beauty, or the perfect mate

- believing they are superior and can only be understood by or associate with equally special people

- requiring constant admiration

- having a sense of entitlement or expecting special favors and unquestioning compliance with their expectations

> One characteristic of a person with narcissistic personality disorder is they lack empathy for others.

- taking advantage of others to get what they want

- having an inability or unwillingness to recognize the needs and feelings of others

- being envious of others and believing others envy them

- behaving in an arrogant or haughty manner.

Your parents may have had some narcissistic tendencies, but would not be considered to have narcissistic personality disorder. As with many psychological issues, there is a continuum. Some people would be at the mild end and others at the personality-disordered end of the continuum. Growing up with a parent who falls anywhere on this continuum can be difficult and painful.

Either mothers or fathers can be narcissistic. To simplify matters, I will use the example of a narcissistic mother. If you grew up with a narcissistic mother, you may have realized at some point in your childhood, or early adulthood, that your life was less important to her than her life. In fact, she hardly saw you as a separate person. To her, you were just an appendage, sort of like another arm. Because of this, if you did something she didn't like, she would become angry with you, because, after all, an arm should do the bidding of the person who owns it, right? Perhaps she wouldn't show her anger, but would make you pay for it somehow. Maybe she would make you feel guilty for "hurting her," or blame you for being wrong, or berate you for being stupid, cruel, arrogant, or any number of negative characteristics. She had no empathy for your feelings and didn't really acknowledge you had needs of your own. You were primarily put on earth to serve her.

How might this have affected you?

- You grew up without the unconditional love all children crave.

- You were made to feel you had to earn love, affection, and acceptance.

- When you were a child, you took care of your mom, at least emotionally, instead of her taking care of you.

- You acted like your mom's friend instead of her child; therefore you knew things about her life a child shouldn't know. For example, she told you personal information about her relationship with your father.

- As an adult, you walk on eggshells around her, trying not to upset her, or draw attention to yourself, your needs, or your accomplishments.

- You might still take responsibility for your mom's emotional state, such as changing your behavior around her to keep her happy.

> As an adult child of a narcissistic mother, you might:
>
> - Walk on eggshells around her
> - Take responsibility for her emotions
> - Apologize for things out of your control

- Even as an adult you apologize for things that aren't your fault or aren't in your control.

- You have an ongoing internal monologue that says, "I need to . . . " or, "I should . . . " or, "I have to . . . "

- You are very hard on yourself when you are not able to perform a role or task perfectly.

Healing from a childhood with a narcissistic mother will take five steps, which follow. Journal exercises, such as those I suggest through much of this book, will help with this journey.

Step One: Accept Your Mother's Limitations

Journal Your Journey

Regardless of whether your mother is still in your life, you will need to mourn the loss of your ideal mother. Don't deny the pain of living with a narcissistic mother. Write in your journal what an ideal mother would have been for you. Then, write what growing up with your mother truly was like. Now you can be honest with yourself about what you have lost by having a mother who cared more for her needs than yours.

Perhaps the idea that your mother was incapable of real love and empathy is shocking to you. Maybe you feel guilty for even considering the idea. Here is an example: a music tutor hands a four-year-old a violin and expects her to play a Mozart concerto. The tutor might feel disappointed, angry, and shamed she cannot teach the child to play the concerto, until she realizes the student is incapable of the task. Like the child in this example, most narcissists are incapable of giving authentic love and empathy. Once you accept that your own mother had, or has, this limited capacity, you will be on the road to healing the pain you've experienced in your childhood.

> Once you accept your mother's limited ability to feel authentic love and empathy, you will be on the road to healing.

Step Two: Process Your Feelings

(Don't skip this step, or step three won't work.)

I'm sure you won't be surprised when I advise you to mourn the loss of your ideal of a perfect, loving, caring mother. Every child deserves a mother (or father) who loves her unconditionally, thinks she is the most special child in the world, and would give up anything for her. This is the way God designed families to work. Your mother was unable to love you fully because *something was broken inside her*, not because something was wrong with you. She may have been a victim of her own childhood abuse or experienced trauma she was unable or unwilling to process. Take the time to be honest about your feelings of anger, sadness, and loss.

Doll Therapy

Journal Your Journey

Use your journal for this exercise.

I recommend what Dr. McBride calls "doll therapy."[47] I did this, and I loved it. Go shopping and find a doll that looks like you did between the ages of three and eight. Make sure you love the doll you choose. Bring her home and spend time talking to her. Put her on your bed, favorite chair, or couch, wherever you will see her often. Begin to mother her. Give her the love and attention you didn't get from your own mother. Ask her what she needs from you now.

Write in your journal the things that come to mind. Begin at a young age, and slowly "grow her up." Ask her what she missed out on in her pre-school, elementary, middle school, high school, and even young adult years. Perhaps you wish your mother had been emotionally there for you when friends were mean to you in middle school, when you had your first boy-friend, decided what to do after high school, and birthed your first child.

I enjoyed "mothering myself" in this way. I kept my doll on a chair I sit in to spend time with Jesus every morning. One morning, I saw a sticky note (in my second husband's handwriting!) that said, "What a wonderful little girl you are, so smart and funny." A few days later, another note appeared that read, "You is kind, you is smart, you is important." (This line is from one of my favorite movies, The Help.[48]*) I've kept those notes there for more than a year, allowing them to remind myself I now have unconditional love in my life.*

Step 3: Understand Why You Have Struggled Separating from Her

Children of healthy mothers begin to separate from them around age two. This is when a child begins saying "no!" and "mine!" These mothers allow their children to separate from them gradually and naturally. Children of narcissistic mothers never learn to fully separate from them. An ignored child continues to try to fill her need for love by trying to merge with her mother like an infant. Conversely, a child who is engulfed by mother is not allowed to have her own needs, wants, opinions, or feelings. Neither the ignored nor the engulfed child gets her needs met, nor is she really able to develop a sense of herself apart from her mother.

Have you separated from your mother? One way to tell is to ask yourself if you speak negatively to yourself. Do you often think, "I'm not good enough," or "I'm not strong enough"?

In order to separate from your mother now, you will need to understand how she projects her negative feelings onto you, understand and cope with her envy of you, and eradicate negative self-talk. Let's explore these three.

Her Negative Feelings

Narcissists appear to be very self-confident. In reality, they are the opposite. Deep down, they loathe themselves, but don't want to—or can't—recognize the pain of that feeling. To deal with it, they project this feeling onto those close to them. This is why your mother often criticized (or still does criticize) you. She is projecting the negative things she believes about herself onto you. As a child, you most likely internalized and believed these negative lies she told you. Now, they have most likely become part of what you think about yourself. Understand and accept that this unfair projection was placed on you.

> Though narcissists appear very self-confident, in reality they loathe themselves.

Envy

Though she doesn't show it, your mother is envious of you. She has a very fragile sense of self-esteem. When she sees you succeed in something, it makes her feel bad about herself. The way she feels better about herself is to criticize whatever she feels envious about. For example, perhaps you just bought a house that is bigger than hers. She might criticize the amount of money you "wasted" on it, or the neighborhood it is in, or the "stuck-up" people who live there. In reality, she wishes she lived there.

Negative Self-Talk

If your negative self-talk originated from your narcissistic parent, you might find it helpful to consider the source. Now that you realize your mother has no ability to truly love or have empathy for you, projects her self-loathing onto you, and criticizes you because she envies you, it may be easier for you to logically see she is not a good judge of your character. If that is true, why would you listen to her opinion of you and allow her words to be the internal voice you hear inside your head every day?

> Narcissists have a very fragile self-esteem. When you succeed, she feels bad about herself and even envies you. She criticizes you to feel better about herself.

Step 4: Strengthen Your Internal Being

The Collapse

As a daughter of a narcissistic parent, you may

experience what Dr. McBride calls a "collapse." She describes it as someone popping your "self-esteem balloon." This happens when you feel insulted or invalidated, and it triggers a momentary regression back to your childhood. Old memories of being ignored, demeaned, or humiliated come rushing back, making the current situation feel much bigger than it really is.

> A collapse occurs when an event reminds you of a childhood event where you were ignored, demeaned, or humiliated, and feels like someone has popped your self-esteem balloon.

Does this happen to you? I know it happens to me. My stepkids most frequently cause my collapses. When my stepdaughter turns her head away and pretends she doesn't hear me when I ask her a question, my self-esteem plummets, and I feel completely deflated. Her pretending not to hear me brings me back to the time all my elementary school friends thought it would be "fun" to give me the silent treatment for a month—for no reason.

The Internal Mother/Your Heavenly Father

Dr. McBride suggests using an "internal mother" when you have a collapse. Your internal mother would be your own maternal instinct, the intuitive voice that speaks to you and wants to nurture you and mother you. You may have experienced this when you were mothering the young "you" doll I described earlier in doll therapy.

As Christians, we have an even stronger ally than an internal mother, the Holy Spirit who lives within us. Our heavenly Father, through His Spirit, will strengthen your inner being.

When you feel yourself collapsing, allow your internal mother, or the Holy Spirit, to remind you of your inner worth and how much you are loved. Picture yourself being held within loving arms, and rocked, like a small child. Try not to focus on the event that caused your collapse. Verbally tell yourself your old experience and your current experience are not the same. "That was then, this is now. This is different. I am in control." Focus on being unconditionally loved. You will need that feeling as you move to step 5.

Step 5: Empower Yourself to Set Boundaries with Your Mother

If your mother is on the less severe end of the Narcissistic Personality

Disorder spectrum, you may be able to tell her your feelings about your childhood and how her mothering affected you then and affects you now. You may even consider bringing her into therapy sessions with you (after discussing this with your counselor).

However, most narcissistic mothers will be unwilling or unable to empathize with you enough to look at their behavior in this way. In this case, your best hope of healing will be to set and hold reasonable boundaries with her behavior. Finding a counselor to help you through this process would be wise (see Chapter 6).

How Do You Set Boundaries with Your Mother?

You begin by explaining to your mother what behaviors you are no longer willing to accept. For example, if she calls you every day to tell you how to be a better daughter, you may decide this is too intrusive. You might say to her, "Mom, I have a lot on my plate, and I will only have time to talk to you for twenty minutes one day a week." You can expect her to come back with "How could you?" or "How dare you?" followed by a description of what a terrible, ungrateful daughter you are. Or perhaps she will give you the silent treatment. You want to be prepared for her to react that way and to respond calmly with something like, "I understand this will be a change, and may be difficult for you, but this is what I've decided is best for me right now."

No doubt your mother will call you tomorrow, and she may continue to do so often. (You are wise to simply not answer.) This may go on for the entire week, maybe even for a couple of weeks. However, over time, if you calmly stick to this boundary, she will begin to accept it. If you set boundaries in other areas of your relationship, such as leaving the restaurant where you are having lunch with her if she begins to criticize you, she should begin to treat you with more respect over time.

You Choose the Amount of Contact

You get to decide how much contact you have with your narcissistic mother. Your relationship may range from between relatively close to cordial to businesslike. If your mother is so toxic that having a relationship with her is not worth the strain on your emotions and health, you may decide you need to provide some distance from her life altogether, at least for a time. If she is willing, you can try to reunite with her later, when you feel more emotionally ready to deal with her. Be aware she may not want to reunite with you. You may decide your peace of mind is worth that risk.

What If Your Mother Is Dead?

If your mother is no longer living, you will obviously not need to set boundaries with her. But you may desire to write her a letter, describing your feelings toward her. You can then destroy the letter or symbolically "mail" it to her by putting it at her gravesite.

> You get to choose how much contact to have with your mother. If she is very toxic, you may decide to have no relationship with her.

Summary

Growing up as children of domestic violence can teach many lies about ourselves; these may have influenced us when we chose abusive intimate partners. Instead of minimizing the abuse we suffered (as we may have done as children), facing the truth and feeling the pain of our trauma is a wise choice. Similarly, growing up with a narcissistic parent will leave scars. Facing the truth about our parent(s), and setting boundaries with her or him, will empower us to move into a healthier future.

A Drink of Water
for the Journey

"Children are educated by what the grown-up is, not by his talk."

—CARL JUNG, PSYCHIATRIST

1. If you grew up in a home with domestic violence, which lies did you come to believe about yourself? About others? About God?

2. Have you minimized or denied the abuse you suffered as a child? Why? Did family members intimidate you as a child to keep the abuse secret? What would happen if you stopped denying or minimizing your pain?

3. Did you have a narcissistic parent? In what ways did that affect you as a child, and how does this still affect you?

4. Is it painful to accept your parent's limitations? Did you ever recognize her projecting negative thoughts onto, or envying, you?

5. Does the idea of setting boundaries with your narcissistic parent make you anxious? What are you afraid will happen?

6. Have you ever considered that you get to choose the amount of contact you have with your narcissistic parent? Does this idea give you peace, or make you more anxious?

CHAPTER 6

Seek Counseling

... to bestow on them ... the oil of joy
instead of mourning,
and a garment of praise
instead of a spirit of despair.
—Isaiah 61:3

Perhaps you expected to feel great as soon as you escaped your abuser, and maybe you *did* feel a great sense of relief for a while. However, as time has passed, you may be dismayed by the extent of your emotional pain. This pain might present itself in many ways. Let's explore some of the most common.

Trauma Triggers

What is a trauma trigger? Triggers can be anything that causes a troubling memory in a person who has experienced trauma. You might be having a wonderful day—and then you smell some cabbage. The smell of cabbage instantly brings you back to the day you and your ex ate at an Irish restaurant, and he became enraged when he claimed you were flirting with your waiter. After dinner you had the worst fight of your relationship. The smell of cabbage is innocent and cannot harm you, but the memory of it instantly puts you back to a very traumatic, abusive moment in your past.

Anything can become a trigger: individual people, places, noises, images, smells, tastes, emotions, animals, films, scenes within films, dates of the year, tones of voice, body positions, bodily sensations, weather conditions, time factors, or any combination of the above. Triggers can be subtle, and often are impossible to predict.

I didn't realize I had trauma triggers until recently. My second husband is a gentle man. He often walks quietly into our bedroom while I am brushing my teeth, reading, or listening to music. Often, I don't hear him, and scream before I realize he is there. This bothers him. "Who did you think it was?" he asks. I can't explain my reaction. I just know I am startled, my heart pounds, and I jump a foot.

Recently, I wrote a blog telling the story of how my ex-husband did not speak to me during the entire last year of our marriage . . . unless he snuck up on me to frighten me with surprise rages. I would think I was blissfully alone in a room; suddenly he would be right next to me, screaming in my ear. My counselor called him "the terrorist." As I wrote the blog, it dawned on me: my second husband's innocent, quiet entrances into our bedroom remind me of my first husband's purposeful terrorizing actions . . . they are triggers for me.

I found out many victims of trauma experience what is called an exaggerated startle response. Everyone becomes startled to some degree by loud noises, by people who appear as if out of nowhere, and by other similar things. However, for those who have experienced trauma, our neurological systems are on red alert. So instead of being mildly responsive to surprises, our body has a larger reaction, as if to say: *Danger, danger!*

Sometimes we also read situations as traumatic or dangerous when they are not. Again, this is because our neurological system has been trained to see danger and react. An example is a smoke alarm. Smoke alarms are wonderful inventions, protecting people and homes. However, a smoke alarm will also go off if it gets a whiff of nonemergency items, like baby powder. As victims of trauma, sometimes our safety alarms go off because we actually do smell smoke or danger. But other times they go off in error, or there was just a harmless interaction. One of the many positive outcomes of healing from trauma is that your body will have less of an exaggerated startle response and read the environment more accurately for danger and safety. After you do your recovery work you will still have triggers, but you will be more aware of them and your reaction to them will be less disruptive to your life.

Surprise triggers can be troubling because we cannot predict or defend ourselves against them. Some triggers are not surprises, and we can avoid them, such as violent movies or restaurants where we used to eat with our exes. But other times, we cannot avoid triggers even when we are aware of them. Again, let's take the example of my stepchildren and when they occasionally give me the silent treatment. Sometimes they are mad at me; sometimes they are just being sullen teenagers. Their actions bring me back to the time when my first husband used withholding tactics to control me. He would not speak to me for weeks, months, or even a year at a time in order to get me to do whatever he wanted. Though my stepkids are not in a position of power over me, their silence brings me back to a very painful time in my life.

> Surprise trauma triggers can be troubling because we cannot predict or defend ourselves against them.

Post-Traumatic Stress Disorder

Some abuse victims may develop Post-Traumatic Stress Disorder (PTSD), which is an anxiety disorder. Symptoms of PTSD include: flashbacks of the abuse you've suffered (and feeling as if you are actually experiencing the abuse); traumatic nightmares; avoidance of memories or discussion about your abuse, but memories come back against your will when you are triggered, or by nightmares; diminished interest in pre-traumatic significant activities; or change in sleep, concentration, or reactivity.

I list a few symptoms of PTSD to give you an idea of what it is, not to aid in diagnosing it for yourself. Only a licensed mental health counselor can diagnose and treat this disorder. If you have symptoms of PTSD, and they bother you, you might want to seek counseling for diagnosis and treatment. When you call to set up a first appointment you may want to ask the therapist or counselor about their experience in treating victims of abuse to ensure they have both experience and a plan for helping you heal.

As I mentioned above, I get triggered; almost a decade after leaving the relationship, I still have nightmares about my ex-husband. My second husband must wake me because I get very upset in my sleep, whimpering and crying. In my dream, I am screaming and running in terror from my ex. I don't believe I have PTSD, though I do have some of its symptoms.

Five Stages of Grief

Leaving any relationship is a loss, even if it was an abusive relationship. Any time you experience a loss, you may feel grief. Often, we react to grief in ways that seem odd. Elisabeth Kübler-Ross came up with the theory that people experience five stages of grief.[49] She said these steps don't necessarily come in any order, and every person won't experience all of them. Sometimes you will return to a stage more than once.

The first stage of grief is *denial*. In this stage, we often deny having any negative feelings. "I feel fine. Everything is great in my life," you might say. The second stage of grief is *anger*. You may have a burning rage aimed at your ex, at the situation you find yourself in, or at people or things that seem totally unrelated to the abuse you've experienced. The third stage is *bargaining*. In this stage, you try to reason out what has happened. You might say, "If only I had stood up to him when he first began trying to control me, this would have never happened." Or, "If I had lost 50 pounds, he would have loved me more, and wouldn't have been abusive toward me." Or, "I should never have had children with him. If I hadn't, my kids wouldn't have suffered so much." The fourth stage of grief is *depression*, which I will describe in more detail further on. The last stage is *acceptance*. In this stage, you may still feel sadness and regret for the situation, but you move toward being able to live with it. Your emotions don't rule you. You can begin to look toward the future instead of focusing on the past. You begin to have hope.

> The five stages of grief are:
> 1. Denial
> 2. Anger
> 3. Bargaining
> 4. Depression
> 5. Acceptance

This model is very helpful if you remember your life is not a textbook; it is real and healing is an unorganized business. The good news is acceptance is waiting for you at the end of the process.

Anger

Anger is a natural reaction to being abused. Perhaps you are surprised you have not yet been able to feel anger. If you haven't felt angry, it could be because you hid your anger from your abuser for a long time. You may need to give yourself permission to feel angry, or you may need to hear someone you trust give you permission. Perhaps you are afraid that once you become angry you will lose control of yourself. You may feel you will do something to harm your abuser, those you love, or yourself. If you are really frightened, see a counselor.

Maybe you are extremely angry, and your anger frightens you. Feeling angry may be a new experience! You may not know how to deal with these new strong emotions. You may find your anger seems to be taking control of your life. You may spend many of your waking hours planning ways of finding revenge against your abuser. Or, your anger may be spilling out at innocent ones in your life, your coworkers, or your friends and family.

Anger itself is not a problem. It is part of the grieving process, and it should pass after some time. If your anger doesn't decrease, or begins to interfere with your life, it may be a problem. Chapter 8 describes learning to forgive, which may help decrease your anger. If you fear you might actually take revenge on your abuser, or if your anger is hurting others in your life, seek counseling.

You might try to find some nonharmful ways of expressing your anger. Here are some ideas:

- If you feel like screaming, and there is no one around who might be frightened by your screams, like your children, go ahead and scream! Perhaps you can scream into a pillow to muffle the sounds.

- Hit something soft, like a pillow or stuffed animal.

- Exercise. Sometimes tiring your physical body will release some of the anger.

- Write on paper a list of things that are making you angry. Then, rip up or burn the list.

- Use the energy and motivation that accompanies anger to set up your new life and home.

Although it is good to have positive outlets for your anger, do not stifle it. Allow yourself to experience your anger and own it. Do not be in a hurry to rush through this phase. You may want to tell those close to you (children, close friends, coworkers) that you are experiencing anger due to what you have been through, and you are working hard not to direct your anger toward others. People who love you may be more helpful and grace-filled on those occasions where your anger leaks out toward them if they know what you are working through. You will not be angry forever, but for a time it may be part of your healing journey.

Depression and Thoughts of Suicide

Many survivors of abuse are surprised to find themselves depressed once they leave. Why might you be depressed? Your life should be so much better, shouldn't it? In many ways yes, but as I described in Chapter 3, you have also experienced many losses that you may now need to grieve. While depression is a legitimate stage of grief, if you find yourself stuck in depression for two weeks, you may need counseling.

You may deny feeling depressed. "I don't feel sad," you might say. However, do you have trouble sleeping at night? Do you wake up in the middle of the night and have trouble getting back to sleep, or do you wake very early in the morning? Do you find yourself sleeping too much, or never seem to get enough sleep? Do you eat too much, or have you lost your appetite? Do you feel unable to focus, make even minor decisions, or concentrate on things that used to hold your attention? Do you feel hopeless and believe your life will never improve? Are you thinking about hurting or killing yourself? All of these are signs of depression and may necessitate professional help.

Some signs of depression include:

- Change in sleep habits
- Change of appetite
- Difficulty focusing
- Feeling hopeless
- Thoughts of suicide

If you are considering suicide and feel you are in imminent danger, in the United States[50] call 911 immediately. If you have a suicide plan and have thought through how to act out that plan, head to your nearest emergency room or call 911 immediately. If you are considering suicide, but your danger is less imminent, seek counseling right away.

Exercising good self-care can sometimes relieve mild depression, as I described in Chapter 3. Getting exercise, spending daily time outside in the sun, and spending time with friends and support groups will go a long way toward improving your mood. In addition, working on your relationship with the Lord (Chapter 4) will also help. If these measures don't help your depression, please read on, and look for a counselor.

Self-Harm

Perhaps you feel better when you release your strong emotions by burning, cutting, scratching, banging, or hitting your body parts, picking at your scabs, pulling your hair, or swallowing toxic substances or objects. This is called self-harm.

People around you might assume you do these things in order to get attention. This is usually not the case. In fact, you may go to great lengths to hide the marks you've made because you are embarrassed about what you've been doing. Your guilt about harming yourself may even lead you to harm yourself more, causing a vicious circle. A counselor could help you discern why you feel the need to harm yourself and help you find other, better coping skills.

Addictions

Many abuse victims struggle with addictions. You may be suffering from depression and/or anxiety, and you may use alcohol or drugs to self-medicate. Or perhaps you struggle with a process addiction. (See Chapter 3 for a review of process addictions.) If you are experiencing addiction in response to trauma, it is likely your attempt to cope, or fix a deeper need. You will need help not only in treating the addiction, but also in meeting that deeper need in a healthy way.

Disengaging yourself from these addictions will be difficult, and you cannot do this alone. You will have the best results if you join a support group such as Alcoholics Anonymous, Narcotics Anonymous, Gamblers Anonymous, or Celebrate Recovery. There are many others, depending on your addiction. Be honest with yourself, and seek help immediately.

Do You Need Counseling?

How do you discern whether you need professional counseling? If you can afford it, and you have the time, I recommend it to anyone who has been abused. I strongly recommend professional counseling if you:

- are depressed
- are harming or thinking about harming yourself
- are considering suicide

- plan to physically harm someone else
- feel you have gone backward in your healing process, or you have made no progress for several months
- have extremely painful relationships with loved ones, and they are not improving
- are feeling stuck in your anger or feel frequently fearful.

Many Christians feel like failures if they seek professional counseling. After all, God and the Bible should be all we need, right? *Wrong!* As I explained in Chapter 3, God gave us each other to be His hands and feet here on earth. You do not need to feel ashamed for asking for help after experiencing domestic abuse.

When you are ready, I recommend you work hard to find a skilled counselor. If you can't afford one, look for one who will charge you on a sliding scale fee. This means they will charge you based upon how much you can afford. Some churches will help their members with counseling fees, or they have counselors who are members who will provide treatment for free. Many universities or seminaries offer counseling for a discounted rate, or for free. Many places of employment offer mental health benefits or employee assistance programs as part of their health insurance package. Be persistent: you can receive help with the cost of counseling. If you have tried everything you can think of, and right now find no way to afford individual counseling, try group counseling sessions, which usually cost less than individual sessions. Also, many women's crisis centers offer support groups and hotlines for abuse victims for free. Look around and get the help you can afford.

If you are depressed, you may struggle with keeping your appointments, even if you do find a good counselor. You may be too depressed to go, or you may just want to retreat within yourself, and you begin to talk yourself out of the need to go. However, as Emily Avagliano says in her book, *Dating After Trauma*, "Don't listen to a depressed mind. Don't even indulge it. Just go to a counselor. If the first one does not help, go to a second or third counselor."[51]

When looking for a counselor, pay attention to their skills rather than their religion. A Christian counselor who does not have the skills you need will not help you. Non-Christian counselors will not likely try to talk you out of your faith. If they do, they aren't good counselors; simply

When looking for a counselor, the needed skills are more important than one's religion. A non-Christian counselor might be your best choice.

find another one. As Isaiah 61:5 says:

Strangers will shepherd your flocks; foreigners will work your fields and vineyards.

In other words, non-Christians can bless you if you let them. A friend once put it this way: If your house were on fire, would you ask the fireman if he was a Christian?

Cognitive-Behavioral Therapy

Try to find a counselor who is trained in treating domestic violence and trauma. You have been through trauma, whether your abuse was physical or not. Finding a counselor who uses cognitive-behavioral therapy (CBT) would be wise. CBT is an evidence-based counseling method, which means it has proven effective in countless professional studies. CBT focuses on specific problems and comes up with specific solutions. CBT is based on the theory that what we think affects what we feel and what we feel affects how we act. CBT believes you respond to a situation based on what you believe about yourself, the world, and your future. Also, your core beliefs are shaped by your past experiences, good and bad. These include the abuse, trauma, and neglect you've experienced.

The premise of CBT is that in any event, we have an automatic thought about the event based on our core beliefs. That thought leads to a feeling, which leads to a behavior, and that behavior tends to reinforce our beliefs. The goal of CBT is to challenge our automatic thoughts to see if they are true. If they aren't true, decide what *is* true.

The goal of CBT is to change your core beliefs about yourself, the world, and the future.

This new truth can lead to new feelings and new behaviors. These new behaviors provide new information that can change our core beliefs. Your therapist will help you identify cognitive distortions (wrong thinking patterns) and replace them with truth (facts and truths from the Bible). Learning to challenge your thoughts and replace them with new and healthy ones is hard work. But a good CBT therapist will help you make the changes.

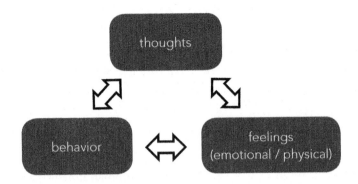

For example, when my stepkids don't respond to me when I speak to them, my automatic thoughts are: *They're ignoring me on purpose; they are treating me like my ex-husband did; they are purposely trying to hurt me; they don't love me; I am unlovable.* When I have these thoughts, I feel worthless, sad, hurt, frightened, and angry. These feelings lead me to withdraw from them, behave passive-aggressively, or begin yelling at them for not speaking to me. All of my behaviors cause distance between us, which then reinforces my core belief that I am unlovable. My husband says, "The more often you hear a lie, the easier it is to believe, but that doesn't make it true."

> The more often you hear a lie, the easier it is to believe, but that doesn't make it true.

In her book, Avagliano says a turning point in her healing occurred when she began not trusting her brain. Instead of believing her thoughts and feelings, she questioned them, talked back to them. She told herself, "A thought is a thought; it is not you."[52] Here are some of the questions she asked herself when she had automatic, negative thoughts.[53]

1. Is this *really* true? Do I need more data before I can accurately draw this conclusion?

2. What other outcomes could occur (when you assume the worst will occur)?

3. Besides giving up, what else can I do to influence this situation in a calm and assertive manner?

4. Am I being a perfectionist?

5. What advice would I give a good friend who told me this? (We often have more compassion for our friends than for ourselves.)

6. Is it realistic? That is, do you expect to have no conflicts your entire life?

7. How long should I suffer this fate? (Even if you do something wrong, how long do you think you should be punished for it?)

8. Is this helpful criticism I am overreacting to? Is this based on one person's opinion?

9. Am I ignoring the good in a situation and only focusing on the bad?

Of course, all of these questions don't apply to every situation. In the case of my stepkids ignoring me, a CBT counselor would help me apply question number one—Is it true? do I need more data before I can accurately draw this conclusion?—to my core belief that I am unlovable. Yes, I have been treated as if I was unlovable by people in my childhood, and by my ex-husband, but does that mean I am unlovable? Today, I have many people in my life who love me: my husband, my friends, my children, and most importantly, Jesus, who loved me enough to die on the cross so I could be with him for all eternity. If God loved me *that* much, I *must* be lovable.

Once I am able to see that I am truly lovable, my feelings about the situation can change. Yes, perhaps my stepkids are ignoring me on purpose; however, that doesn't mean I am unlovable. Therefore, I can decide whether to address their behavior. Perhaps I will ignore it. Perhaps I can lovingly ask them if something is bothering them. The change in my perspective can definitely alter my behavior.

Let's say I lovingly ask my stepdaughter if something is bothering her, and she bursts into tears, lays her head on my shoulder, and begins telling me about how her best friend bullied her at school that day. Her action of sharing her life and pain will begin to change my core belief that I am unlovable.

Eye Movement Desensitization and Reprocessing

In addition to CBT, I also found Eye Movement Desensitization and Reprocessing (EMDR)[54] therapy to be helpful. EMDR is a type of psychotherapy that helps people heal quickly from trauma. Studies have shown that a relatively short treatment using EMDR can be as effective as years of psychotherapy. EMDR therapy demonstrates that the mind can in fact heal from psychological trauma, much as the body recovers from physical trauma.

The therapy works this way: traumatic memories are often stored in the part of the brain that controls emotion. The counselor will stimulate your brain either by making your eyes go back and forth (similar to the Rapid Eye Movement [REM] you experience during sleep), or by delivering a slight pulse, first in one of your hands, then the other, back and forth. He will then ask you to think of a painful memory. Your brain will quickly move from one memory to another, instinctively knowing how to reprocess these memories and heal itself. By moving the sensation in your hands, or your eyes, across the midline of your brain, you are allowing both hemispheres of your brain to be engaged in therapy. The traumatic memory is reprocessed and moved from the emotional part of your brain to the thinking/reasoning part of your brain. This takes away the emotional power of the memory.

> The insights clients gain in EMDR come from reprocessing memories inside their own brain.

With EMDR therapy, trauma victims find that the meaning of the painful events they have suffered are transformed on an emotional level. Victims shift from feeling horror and self-disgust to holding the firm belief, "I survived it and I am strong." Unlike talk therapy, the insights clients gain in EMDR come from reprocessing the memories inside their own brain, rather than from anything the counselor does. The client moves quickly from feeling debased by her experiences to feeling empowered.

Psychotropic Medications

What if your counselor believes you should take medications, such as anti-depressants or mood stabilizers? Many Christians struggle with this, believing taking medications for a mental health problem is a sign they are not trusting God enough, or they have somehow failed morally. I don't believe this is true. I believe some of us are predisposed to mental health issues the same way others are predisposed to having high blood pressure or diabetes. Often, mental illness is caused by missing chemicals in the brain, which mood-altering drugs can supply. If you have worked with your counselor to alter your moods via counseling, and you still struggle, your counselor may recommend you see a psychiatrist or medical doctor to determine whether medications might be right for you.

You may need to take medications for several months, a year, or the rest of your life. Either way, do not be dismayed. Remember, Jesus didn't come for the healthy, but for the sick, (Matthew 9:12,13). And as it says in Romans 8:31-39, nothing will separate us from Jesus' love:

What, then, shall we say in response to these things? If God is for us, who can be against us? He who did not spare his own Son, but gave him up for us all—how will he not also, along with him, graciously give us all things? Who will bring any charge against those whom God has chosen? It is God who justifies. Who then is the one who condemns? No one. Christ Jesus who died—more than that, who was raised to life—is at the right hand of God and is also interceding for us. Who shall separate us from the love of Christ? Shall trouble or hardship or persecution or famine or nakedness or danger or sword? As it is written:

"For your sake we face death all day long;

we are considered as sheep to be slaughtered."

No, in all these things we are more than conquerors through him who loved us. For I am convinced that neither death nor life, neither angels nor demons, neither the present nor the future, nor any powers, neither height nor depth, nor anything else in all creation, will be able to separate us from the love of God that is in Christ Jesus our Lord.

Summary

Finding a good counselor can be a process. You will need to find someone who can both challenge and support you in your journey toward healing. Having someone invest in you and supply you with the skills to live a healthy life is worth the investment.

A Drink of Water for the Journey

Without counsel plans fail, but with many advisers they succeed.

Listen to advice and accept instruction, that you may gain wisdom in the future.

—Proverbs 15:22, 19:20, ESV

1. Did you expect to feel differently after you left your abuser? Better or worse than you do now?

2. Do you experience trauma triggers? If so, what types of things trigger you? How do you react?

3. Have you experienced any of the five stages of grief? If so, which ones? Which were most intense for you?

4. Have you struggled with, or do you now struggle with, anger? How have you handled your anger?

5. Have you felt, or do you now feel, depressed? What have you done or can you do to decrease your depression? Are there options from this chapter you might consider?

6. Do you believe seeing a counselor would help you heal from the abuse you've suffered? Why or why not? If so, how might it help?

CHAPTER 7

Seek Healing and Protection for Your Children

*"Their descendants will be known among the nations
and their offspring among the peoples.
All who see them will acknowledge
that they are a people the Lord has blessed."*

—Isaiah 61:9

In my experience, moms will never be truly healed if their kids have not experienced healing. Our lives are so wrapped up in their lives, aren't they? If they suffer, we suffer. Because of this, finding healing for your children is doubly important. You will want to help them heal because you love them, yes. But also, helping them on their journey to healing will help you on *your* journey.

Women who have come out of abusive relationships rarely get the credit they deserve for how hard they've worked to understand their children's difficulties, to help them, and to protect them from exposure to their abuser's behavior. You have already done many things to shield them from your abuser's aggression, or to help them heal, and show them love and affection; making a huge difference in their lives. In this chapter, I will try to build on what you have already started.

When you were with your abuser, he probably did not support your role as a parent; in fact, he probably made it much harder. Most likely, he told you what a terrible parent you

> Give yourself credit for all the ways you have *already* tried to protect and help your children.

were, often in front of your children. And though you know he often lied about you and your capabilities, a part of you may still believe some of these lies. If you struggle with these negative thoughts, Chapter 3 can help you work through them. Getting past these negative beliefs about yourself is paramount; your children need you now.

Affects of Abuse on Your Children

Though you have done everything you could to protect your children, the sad truth is, your children *have* been affected, even if your abuser focused his abuse mainly on you. In order to help your children heal, you will need to accept some difficult truths, without denial.

1. **Your children were more aware of your abuse than you might care to think, even if you tried to hide it.** How do children find out? Many ways: they could tell you were upset; seeing signs of strain in the home; seeing signs of fighting; or seeing or hearing incidents.

2. **Your children have been afraid, even if they never appeared to be.** Because they can tell you are already burdened enough, they may try to hide their fear from you. They previously hid their fear because they didn't want to be punished by your abuser if they showed how afraid they were. Their fear could present itself in many ways, which are outlined in Lundy Bancroft's book *When Dad Hurts Mom: Helping Your Children Heal the Wounds of Witnessing Abuse.*[55] These include overeating or refusing to eat; nail biting, teeth grinding, outbreaks of acne or eczema; frenetic or distracting activity (rocking, tapping, jumping, chewing, or the obsessive need to do sports); developing phobias or compulsive behaviors (fear of monsters or strangers, or needing to wash their hands constantly); retreating into fantasy worlds; sleep disturbances (sleeping in excess, difficulty falling or staying asleep, nightmares,

> Truths you will need to accept:
>
> 1. Your children have been aware of your abuse.
> 2. This abuse has caused them fear.
> 3. Younger children almost always blame themselves for the abuse.
> 4. They interpret the abuse differently than you do.
> 5. Once you are safe, your kids' behavior may surprise you.

night terrors, night talking, or night walking); or regressive behavior (potty "accidents," clinging to "lovies").

Sometimes children with ADHD will be put on medication, which might be helpful, but they should more correctly be viewed as trauma survivors who need safety and healing more than medication. Sometimes children's fear and trauma responses can look quite similar to yours!

3. **Younger children almost always think they are to blame for the abuse.** "If I had only picked up my toys, Dad wouldn't have gotten so mad," or, "If I had been a better girl, Dad and Mom would still be married." Children will often choose one of two extremes when they feel guilty about causing the abuse or divorce. They will become the "perfect" child and excel in school, sports, or church activities, or they will become the "bad" child. This child will do everything possible to prove just how bad he or she is, and fail at school, get in trouble with the law, or act out at home. The perfect child is trying to do everything possible to prevent the abuser from finding fault with you and her in order to limit the number of abusive outbursts. The bad child behaves badly subconsciously to bring all the abuser's negative attention to him and away from you, to protect you.

Children's beliefs that they caused the abuse or can control/decrease/stop it can be both hurtful to the child and also developmentally appropriate. Children are supposed to be narcissistic and engage in magical thinking to a certain extent. If something good happens in their life, they often believe it is because they wished it to be, or because they are so good or smart. This can make life feel exciting. However, the flip side of this is they often believe they cause negative things that occur in their world. Even kids in elementary school who will first tell you they did not cause their parents' divorce will often later confide that they still feel like it is their fault.

You can help your children by frequently telling them the abuse was not their fault. Let them know your abuser is entirely responsible for his actions, no matter what others do around him. Let them know that adults do not get to blame their behavior on their children.

4. **Children interpret the abuse in ways that may not make sense to you.**

- They may say, "I heard if your dad hits your mom, police come and put you all in jail," or, "Mommy was crying because I didn't do what Daddy told me to do, and then he yelled at her and called her a bad name. She's very angry with me for making Daddy yell at her like that."[56]

- They may tell stories from the past, but their version is vastly different from reality. In the stories they may make the family sound as if things were ideal when you and your abuser were together. They are romanticizing the family concept as they grieve the loss of their family. I was surprised during my divorce when my kids described life in our home as "Our parents were always mad at each other," rather than the way I saw it: "Whenever Dad doesn't get what he wants, he gives Mom the silent treatment."

5. **Once you have left your abuser and have experienced some peace, your children may react in surprising ways.**

   - They may begin to feel safe to act out the trauma they have experienced. Children who previously acted "perfectly" to prevent the abuser from harming you and them may now begin to act disrespectfully. They may show the anger, sadness, and confusion they hid for so long.

   - They may begin to idolize their father. Once they no longer live with the daily abuse, they may forget how badly he used to behave. If they rarely see him, they may miss him, even though he was not a kind person when they lived with him. The memory of his abuse is fading; they begin to see him in a different light.

   - Even though they may realize their father was abusive, they will feel caught in the middle between the two of you, their loyalties divided. They may begin keeping secrets from you or be reluctant to tell you things their father has said.

These truths may be painful to think about, but don't shrink back. There will be a lot you can do to help your children heal once you understand what they've suffered. Remember, *you* are not responsible for the abuse they suffered; that responsibility lies with your abuser. However,

you are the best person to help them heal, because no one else will step up to do this, especially not your abuser. He will probably forever
deny he has done any harm to any of you.

> You are not
> responsible for
> the abuse they've
> suffered—but
> you are the best
> person to help
> them heal.

Rebuilding Your Children's Trust

Helping your children will be easier if they
trust you completely. However, your abuser
probably spent a lot of time and energy wearing you down in the eyes of
your children. He made them believe his bad treatment of all of you was
your fault. He may have also told them he loved them and you don't, that
you were stupid, and much more. By his actions, they realized he was the
one with power in the relationship, and you were less powerful, so they
may not believe you can protect them from him. You will need to rebuild
the trust that he has torn down. How can you do this? I recommend you
look at Ephesians 6:1-4, which says:

> *Children, obey your parents in the Lord, for this is right.*
> *"Honor your father and mother"—which is the first commandment*
> *with a promise—"so that it may go well with you and that you*
> *may enjoy long life on the earth."*
>
> *Fathers, do not exasperate your children; instead,*
> *bring them up in the training and instruction of the Lord.*

Here are some keys to practically live out these verses with your kids.

Children, Respect Your Parents

First, you will need to reinstate yourself as the authority figure in your
home. This may seem strange since you have all recently left your controlling abuser. However, if your children do not see you as the loving
leader of your home, they will never feel safe, nor will they trust you. If
you are not the leader of your single-parent home, who will be? Your
kids? Your abuser from afar? Either of these is a prescription for disaster.

If your abuser was the main disciplinarian and now you need to fill that
role in order to gain respect, let your children know changes are coming
and why. Your children will adapt better if you tell them in advance.
Also, work to change their hearts, not just their behavior. Let them know
you love them, and that God's plan is for families to work together, with

the parents (you in this case) as the loving leader of the home.

Your kids may have begun treating you with disrespect, as your abuser used to. You will need to require respect from them. Don't permit sarcasm, noises of disgust, or insulting hand motions or facial expressions. Also, don't allow them to ignore you. If they do, give them a meaningful consequence. For example, if your child ignores you when you ask her to clean her room, she may not get to play when her best friend comes over. Explain to her in a loving way that each person in the house has to help each other, that it is disrespectful for family members to ignore each other. Then tell her that in order to help her remember this, you are going to ask her to spend the time she would have spent playing with her friend cleaning her room. Offer to help her. Then ask her to help you with a chore you need to do.

> You need to be the loving leader of your single-parent home.

My husband reminds me when I am frustrated with his kids to *bring them close* instead of *pushing them away*. What does he mean by that? When I am angry with my stepkids, my knee-jerk reaction is to want to send them back to their mom's house. He challenges me to push past this feeling and try to win their hearts. Yes, I need to require them to respect me as a parental figure in our home, but I also need to let them know I love them. If I know one loves quality time, I might ask her to bake cookies with me. If I know another appreciates words of affirmation, I will search for *something* I can compliment her for. You would be surprised what a difference this makes in our home.

Taking back the respect you deserve will take some time, and lots of energy, but it will be worth it for all of you.

Parents, Don't Exasperate Your Children

1. **Get healing for all of you.** You have already started doing this by reading and following the advice in this book. Seek counseling for you and your children if possible. Surround yourself and your children with healthy people who will enrich your lives.

2. **Admit when you are wrong, and apologize to your children.** Be open with them, but don't use them as your confidants. They are children, not your friends. Find friends to share your pain with. Let your kids be kids.

3. **If you are addicted to any substances, work hard to get off them right away.** Then work equally hard to stay off them. You will not be able to be the best parent you can be if you are addicted to drugs or alcohol. In addition, your children will not be able to trust you or depend on you. Similarly, if you have any process addictions (anything done repeatedly and to excess; review Chapter 3), you will need to work to free yourself from these as well. Seek an appropriate support group, and begin your journey to freedom from your addiction *today.*

4. **Believe them if they tell you about abusive things your ex is doing to them, or has done in the past.** You may be tempted to discount or ignore them when they tell you about further abuse they are suffering from him, especially if this happens on court-ordered visits, and you might feel you cannot protect them from him. You can consider reporting his actions to Social Services, the police, or a custody evaluator if you have one on your case. Sometimes these actions will be helpful, and sometimes they will backfire on you. (We'll talk more about this later in this chapter.) However, even if you decide reporting his actions will not help and you think you can't do anything about his behavior right away, you should believe your children and give them your emotional support. They need to know someone cares about their troubles. Children can cope with many difficult things if they know they have at least one adult in whom they can confide and trust.

5. **Ask yourself how you can make your kids feel you are a safe haven for them.** Think of yourself as having loving arms you can wrap around them at all times, even when they are far from you. Can you send a special toy, blanket, or picture of yourself with them when they are visiting him? Can you call them at the same time each day when you are apart so they know you are thinking of them? What routines can you instill in your home that can give them a sense of stability and peace? What prayers or songs can you teach them so they can comfort themselves when they are away from you?

6. **Don't spank your kids.** In many cultures, this is an acceptable form of discipline. However, spanking will only further traumatize children who have been abused or who have seen you being abused. It also tells them violence is justifiable in families as long as it is

"for your own good." You will want to do everything you can not to reinforce this belief in your family. Find alternative forms of discipline. These can include: taking away privileges; restricting movement (timeouts for younger kids, or determining a "boring spot" they must sit in for a minute for every year of age); having them do extra chores around the house (join them in those chores for extra bonding); or docking an allowance. Try to match the consequence as closely as possible to the offense so the child can understand the discipline.

7. **Read books on parenting during your divorce, and join a support group with your children if possible.** Many women's crisis centers have groups for victims and their children. Or, join a divorce support group in your church or community.

Fighting Against the Continuing Negative Influence of Your Abuser

Helping your children heal would be much simpler if they had no contact with your abuser. However, if your abuser is also their father, chances are good the court system will award some unsupervised contact with him. In my case, my ex asked for and received week on/week off parenting time with our children. With your abuser's continued presence in their lives, you can expect your children's healing to be more complicated than it would otherwise be.

In Chapter 2 I described numerous ways your abuser might use your children to continue abusing you; it's important that you review those items. In that chapter I also provided many ideas on how you can set boundaries around his behavior to keep yourself physically and emotionally safe. Besides the specific advice I gave in that chapter, what can you do if your abuser behaves in these destructive ways? Here are more options.

1. **Limit the amount of time your children spend with your abuser as much as you possibly can.** The more time they spend with him, and the closer they become with him, the more difficult their healing process will be. You probably instinctively want to keep your kids from your abuser, but your children may miss their father so much you feel sorry for them. If he begins fading into the background of

their lives, don't go out of your way to increase their contact with him, no matter how much pain this causes them in the short term. In the long term, they will be better off. If your abuser is not your children's biological or adoptive father, you are not obligated to permit visitation. As Proverbs 22:10 says:

> Drive out the mocker, and out goes strife;
> quarrels and insults are ended.

2. **Make your relationship with your children the best it can be.** Now is the time to invest in their lives. Yes, I'm aware many concerns are begging for your attention now, such as your own emotional and physical health and finding a job and safe place to live. However, pour whatever energy and time you can into your kids while also remembering to take care of yourself (Chapter 3). Put dating on hold; starting a relationship with another man will funnel away any spare time and attention you might have given to your children. Studies[57] have proven that a close relationship with their mother is the best indicator of health for children coming out of abuse.

3. **Don't speak against their father, but do listen to any concerns they share.** If you bad-mouth their father, your kids will feel they need to defend him. However, if they come to you with problems, let them know you understand their concerns. Given your feelings about their father, you will probably have a difficult time holding your tongue and not sharing your own negative thoughts about him. This won't help them. Try to simply acknowledge their feelings—and keep yours to yourself. Deal with your own fears and emotions separately, either with a friend or a counselor. If you have real concerns for their safety, ask someone you trust to help you decide whether to do something about your fears, such as calling the police, Social Services, or a custody evaluator.

> If you speak negatively about their father, your kids will feel they need to defend him.

4. **Prepare for court intervention even if you don't expect you will need to.** Often, an abuser will pretend to go along with the custody plan you desire, only to surprise you later by calling you into court unexpectedly. Better to be safe than sorry. Be prepared with a dia-

ry of important events; save letters, emails, texts, and handwritten notes from him. Keep a record of his behavior and any police intervention you have had. Ask friends to be ready to give testimony about abuse they have witnessed, especially as it involved the children. Find a lawyer if you can afford it, especially one who specializes in custody battles. Educate yourself on what to expect from the judges in your district.

Helping Your Children Heal

The most powerful gift you can give your children is to pray for them. My prayer partner Janet reminds me often that there is no such thing as a perfect parent. You can do everything "right" and "by the book" and still have children that rebel, because, as Romans 3:23 says, *we all have sinned and fall short of the glory of God.* Every person on earth has free will. All we can do as parents is try to be faithful, do our best, and remember God is the one who changes hearts, including our own.

When my first husband and I raised our kids, we made many mistakes. I wasn't as faithful as I should have been in praying for them because my own life was such a mess. However, God filled in the gaps for me. My children have all grown to be strong followers of the Lord, and they have made wise choices. God did immeasurably more than I could ever have asked or imagined (Ephesians 3:20).

Keep in mind parenting is a process. You will grow in your parenting just as your kids will grow to adulthood. Don't be overwhelmed by the numerous suggestions I or others provide for helping your children heal; simply begin to incorporate them slowly into your life as a family. You will be surprised how much you can accomplish over time if you are patient with yourself and your kids.

According to Lundy Bancroft and his book *When Dad Hurts Mom,* the key elements to helping children heal from abuse are:[58]

- A close relationship with you

- Safety

- Good relationships with siblings

- A healthy self-esteem

- Connection to other loved ones, to peers, to self, and to God

- Opportunities to talk about events and express their feelings
- Opportunities to release distressing feelings
- Information about abuse
- Empowering them.

I've talked a lot about helping your kids have a close relationship with you. Let's cover some other vital topics.

Safety

If your children are still in contact with your abuser, their lives won't be as safe as you would like them to be. You can strive to make their lives in your home as safe as possible. Use good boundaries with your ex to keep him out of your home. These might include changing your locks, changing your telephone number, moving, and/or getting a restraining order. He should not be allowed to enter your home—ever. (I will have more on safety planning later in this chapter.)

In addition, make sure you are as safe a person as you can be. As we have said, work hard to stop any addictions. If you have trouble with depression or anxiety, get good counseling (Chapter 6). If you find yourself raging at your kids or losing patience with them often, search for a parenting support group in your church or community.

Good Relationships with Siblings

Siblings can be a great source of support, or another source of abuse in families, depending on the quality of the relationships. If your children have learned to treat each other as their father used to treat them, you will need to help them unlearn these behaviors. Just as your kids need to learn to treat you with respect, you must also insist they treat each other with respect. This doesn't mean they must always "love" each other. That would be unrealistic and fake. Allow them to be angry, but teach them how to resolve conflict without violence or put-downs. Don't feel you must always be in the middle, solving every conflict for them. Give them room to argue and come to resolutions by themselves in respectful ways.

> Siblings can be a great comfort or another source of abuse.

Healthy Self-Esteem

Help your children have a healthy self-esteem. Up to this time, it probably has been either very low or highly inflated by their abusive father. Don't compare them to their siblings or other family members, and especially not to their father! Don't pigeonhole them by saying, "Sally is the sweet one, and John is the smart one." Sally may not always want to be sweet, and John may not always be the smartest kid in his class. Let them explore all the facets of who they can be. If they are feeling down, don't immediately try to brush their feelings aside. Instead, ask them why they feel this way. Let them learn to express their feelings in words, even if their feelings make you uncomfortable at times. Allow them to do physical activities that will release their stress, including jumping, running, or playing sports.

Connections to Other Loved Ones and Peers, a Church Community, and God

Loved ones and peers: Encourage your kids to have relationships with loving family members and other safe adults in their lives. If family members are far away, have them write, call, even Skype or FaceTime their loved ones. Give your kids opportunities to play with other children their age.

Church community: Find a church community in which you can all feel comfortable. You all need other believers to support you now. As it says in Hebrews 10:24, 25:

> *And let us consider how we may spur one another on*
> *toward love and good deeds, not giving up meeting together,*
> *as some are in the habit of doing, but encouraging one another—*
> *and all the more as you see the Day approaching.*

Churches that are extremely patriarchal may reinforce the chauvinistic ideas their father began teaching them. Instead, try to find a church that will support all of you, one that respects every person in the family, no matter the life circumstance.

To God: Teach your children to pray. When times are rough, such as when they are with their father and apart from you, they can draw great comfort from feeling God near. Help them learn to love the Bible. You can make this a fun dinnertime activity. Jim Weidmann and Curt Bruner have created a wonderful series called the Family Night Tool Chest.[59] The books in this series have fun activities using common household items that underscore truths from the Bible. Or, you can choose one Bible verse, read it aloud, and ask your kids what they think it means. Memorizing the verse together will help store God's Word in their hearts. If you teach the verses by putting them to music, they will be easier to remember. You can find many CDs and YouTube videos with Bible verses put to music.

Opportunities to Talk About Events and Express Their Feelings

Kids need many opportunities to talk about traumatic events. They may need to talk about the same event over and over. Others may not want to talk about them at all and will need to be encouraged, possibly with a counselor. Others may not be able to talk about them, but will be able to show what has happened through drawings.

Your children may have very mixed feelings about their father. They may be afraid of him but miss him at the same time. They may love him but also hate him. If they say something like, "I hate him, and I want to kill him!" try not to be shocked, and talk them out of their feelings. If they try to hide their bitter feelings, they will begin to think their feelings are who they are, rather than just what they feel. Strong, conflicting emotions can be confusing to kids. Better to help them label and own what they are feeling.

Opportunities to Release Distressing Feelings

Adults often learn to hide their feelings. Your children will heal more quickly if you allow them to release those feelings they had likely been hiding while you were all living with your abuser. You may not enjoy it when they begin releasing them, because they may begin having long crying spells, temper tantrums, raging fits, screaming, or hysterical laughter. You may also be dismayed that your kids seem to be "fine," "happy," and "normal" when they visit your ex, and then lose it the minute they return to your house. This may actually be a good sign! They are putting on a show at his house, even though they may actually feel upset, fearful, or angry. When they get to your house they feel safe enough to release all their distressing feelings. Allow them to do this. The more you allow them to do it in a

> Children heal faster when given a chance to release their distressing feelings with:
>
> • Long crying spells
> • Temper tantrums
> • Raging fits
> • Screaming
> • Hysterical laughter

loving environment, the sooner they will heal.

What should you do while your child is throwing a tantrum or having a crying fit? You may be tempted to yell at your child to stop, or to ignore him. If you treat these as healing events during which you lovingly stand by to make sure your child doesn't hurt himself, you may be surprised how he will come out of these times feeling relieved and refreshed, ready to cooperate with you. Tantrums and deep crying are both natural emotional healing processes in children.[60]

Information About Abuse

Free them from any guilt feelings they might unreasonably hold. Explain the dynamics of abuse; use age-appropriate language. They still love their father, but let them know your abuser is responsible for his abusive actions; your children didn't cause them.

Empowering Your Children

Give them a voice

When you lived with your abuser, you often had to stifle your feelings and thoughts in order to keep yourself safe from his rages. Your kids probably have learned to do the same. When they are with their father, they must agree with him in order to keep the peace. They cannot be their true selves. One of the best things you can do to empower them is to help them learn to have a voice of their own. What does this look like?

1. Listen to their feelings, opinions, and ideas, and take them into account when you make parenting decisions. I always struggled with this, until I read a book, by Scott Brown, called *How to Negotiate with Kids . . . Even When You Think You Shouldn't: Seven Essential Skills to End Conflict and Bring More Joy into Your Family.*[61] This book helped me loosen the reigns on my kids a little, and it allowed me to let them grow up to be the people God meant them to be. I recommend it.

2. Allow them to fight their own battles. Don't rush to fix every problem they face outside your home. Instead, help them problem-solve at home. Give them the tools they might need to deal with an issue. Step in only if the problem gets worse, if it seems your child cannot handle it or is in danger.

3. Encourage them to write letters to your local newspaper or elected

officials about issues they care about. Or help them volunteer for causes they believe in: save their money and give to aid the fight against human trafficking; run a 5K for various causes, like cancer research; or make lunches for the local rescue mission.

4. Praise them for standing up for their friends and siblings when they are mistreated.

5. Teach them the difference between assertive and aggressive. You want your children to be assertive, to know what they believe, and to stand up for themselves and others. But they do not have to be aggressive to get what they want. Your abuser may provide an aggressive example, but children need to learn being assertive is the healthier way to live.

Critical thinking

Another great way to help your kids is to teach them to think critically about the way their father manipulates them. This will not be easy since you don't want to openly speak negatively about him. How can you do this? Look to the media and other life situations for teachable moments. There are many examples of music videos and movies that show "real men" mistreating, abusing, and even forcing sex on "their women." If your children are involved with sports, you will have ample opportunities to see parents screaming at their kids from the sidelines. When these examples occur, you can tell your kids what *you* think, but perhaps even better, ask them how this type of behavior makes *them* feel. Ask them how they would feel if someone treated them that way. Then brainstorm together about ways adults can handle things better.

> You can teach children to understand their father's manipulation with examples from other parents, music videos, movies, even TV commercials.

Television commercials also provide teachable moments that may not be as obvious. A car commercial is designed to make you believe they want to give you freedom, but what are they really after? Your money! What is the hair care commercial trying to tell you? If you buy their product, you will get men to love you, right? *Wrong!* You get the idea.

Once your kids learn to think critically, they will also be able to see through some of their father's manipulation tactics. When he tells them,

"I do what I do for our family," he really means, "I do what I do for me."

Safety planning

If your children are required to go to unsupervised visits with your ex, and they, or you, are afraid for their safety, you should consider safety planning. This planning helps them remain safe when their father is in the explosive stage of the abuse cycle. Here are some ideas that can help them:[62]

- Teach them your phone number, including the area code

- Suggest they leave his home when he begins to be violent or shows signs he might be (such as when he starts drinking), and run to neighbors who know about the abuse

- Lock themselves in a bedroom, preferably one with a telephone, and call you or 911

- Arrange a code word with you, friends, or relatives so they can use the phone to call for help without their father knowing what they are doing

- If you are concerned he might try to abduct them, rehearse with your children their full name, the town and state you live in, and how to call 911. Discuss strategies for passing written messages to other adults to indicate they are being abducted, or to leave messages in public restrooms (especially women's rooms, where your abuser is unlikely to go).

If you are in the middle of a custody battle with your ex, he may use the fact that you have talked with your kids about safety planning against you. In this case, try to get a professional, such as a therapist or domestic violence advocate, to aid in the safety planning.

A Word of Caution About Custody

You may find taking care of your hurting children difficult and stressful. You might be considering allowing their father to have full custody of them, just for a brief time, while you work on your own healing, thinking you will get them back when you feel better. I advise you to resist this temptation if at all possible. Chances are good, once you have assented to such a decision, you will not be able to get your children back

Stand Up for Your Children in Court if Necessary

I had a poor experience with the court system when I separated from my abusive husband. Since then, I have heard other survivors' stories that were worse than mine; if you've read my blog, you know this is a hot button for me.

General Beliefs Held By Court Personnel

The days when the courts assumed children of divorce were better off with their mothers are gone. Instead, the pendulum has swung the other way, and the norm is for parents to split custody (or "parenting time") equally, or for fathers to be given more time than mothers in contested custody battles. This can be true even if domestic violence existed in the relationship. Why? There are several reasons:

1. Family court judges are generally uneducated about domestic violence. They assume, incorrectly, that once the relationship ends, the violence ends.

2. Judges assume that children need their parents equally, no matter how much time the children spent with each parent before the divorce. So, for example, the court may not care that the mother did 90 percent of the child care before the divorce and the father 10 percent. They would still assume 50/50 custody would be "best for the children."

> Courts no longer assume children of divorce are better off with their mothers.

3. In general, judges (even women judges) are prejudiced against women, especially domestic violence survivors. This is because domestic violence survivors often make allegations of abuse against their former partners, which judges don't consider important. Often, women survivors are suffering from PTSD and make poor witnesses while their abusers appear more confident and emotionally stable.

4. Many judges believe abused mothers regularly lie about the abuse they and their children have experienced in order to keep the children from their fathers. This is a theory called Parental Alienation Syndrome that Richard Gardner termed in the 1980s. It claims a parent can alienate a child from the other parent, usually as part of a

custody battle. Many abusive fathers use this theory to explain why protective mothers try to limit their exposure to their children.

5. Because many fathers of divorce abandon their kids, judges are often reluctant to limit a father's access to his children.

Protecting Yourself and Your Children in the Family Court System

Given the way the family court system currently handles divorce in cases of domestic violence, you would be wise to prepare yourself for a potential court battle with your ex. Here are some tips that might prove helpful.

Present yourself as a stable, caring parent

Because courts tend to be biased against women, do everything you can to present yourself as a well-balanced, caring parent. Be careful what you say in front of *anyone* from the court, including lawyers, judges, custody evaluators, Social Services, and police officers. You know your ex's character and parenting are lacking, but talking about this in your custody case will not serve you well. Be able to articulate why your ex's past abuse makes you afraid *for your children*. Focus on their well-being. Try to help the court gain an understanding of your abuser's mental and emotional state, as well as the long-lasting effects this has had and is having on your children. This will help eliminate the court's perspective that you are "out to get" your ex or are a silly paranoid woman.

Try not to appear to "alienate" your children from your ex

Although a recent study[63] found fathers were three times more likely than mothers to attempt to alienate their children, most court personnel still believe mothers are the ones who lie and try to keep helpless, loving dads away from their children. Because of this, the court may dismiss any report you make of abuse your ex perpetrates against your children. Even if your children report their father has sexually abused them, the court may not believe them. Do everything in your power not to appear to be alienating your children. If you must make a report, focus on the well-being of your children, not on the poor character of your ex.

> Courts are biased *against* mothers. Therefore, do whatever you can to present yourself as a reasonable and caring parent.

Gather as much concrete evidence of his abuse as you can
Examples include:

- Police reports you've made

- Restraining orders you have/had against your ex

- Psychological evaluations on you, your abuser, or your children

- Reports written by a forensic psychologist regarding your children's mental health

- Medical records

- Pictures of bruises on you or your children, or damaged property in your home (pictures taken by police usually carry more weight)

- Letters from friends, neighbors, or family members describing abuse they've seen or heard

- Letters from teachers, coaches, pastors, counselors, or anyone who might have knowledge of things your ex has done or said to your children.

Any or all will help you demonstrate his abuse is not just your word against his.

Keep a record
Keep a record of your children's lives in a notebook. Write down *everything* that happens, along with the date and time it happened. Write when you or your ex dropped off or picked the children up, along with any communication you had with your ex (text, email, phone, or in person). Write about any time you spoke to your kids over the phone while they were with your ex. This record will be invaluable to you during a possible custody battle. You will have proof, in your own handwriting, of everything that you and your ex have done or not done for and with your kids. He will be less likely to accuse you of bad parenting if you have this complete record.

Educate yourself about the judges and other members of the court
Every court district and officer of the court has its own prejudices. On the Internet, you can find the ruling record of the judges in your district. You can ask the domestic violence advocates at your local women's crisis center what other victims have experienced in family court. Are some judges more helpful to women; are there others you will want to avoid at

all costs? Is there one lawyer who consistently wins his hearings before these judges? The better prepared you are, the better your results might be.

Be careful when dealing with a custody evaluator

Custody evaluators are sometimes called guardian ad litems, child and family investigators (CFIs), or child advocates. These are lawyers or mental health practitioners assigned by the court or hired by the divorcing parents to decide how much custody each parent should receive. Unfortunately, most of these evaluators are not domestic violence advocates and therefore often make the same incorrect assumptions judges make in these cases.

They will often interview each parent and decide custody based on which parent seems most truthful. If they are mental health practitioners they may also give each parent a psychological evaluation. The problem with these methods is that abusers have the ability to look mentally healthy to outsiders, i.e., to those they aren't abusing. They can appear charming, intelligent, and caring.

Abused women, on the other hand, often appear angry, depressed, and/or suffering from PTSD. Because of this, the custody evaluator may decide *you* are the person with the problem; they see you as less stable, and thus a less fit parent.

> Custody evaluators are not usually trained in domestic violence—even if they claim to be. Work to impress them. They are not your friends.

In his book *When Dad Hurts Mom*, Lundy Bancroft recommends you not request or accept a custody evaluator on your case unless you know who the evaluator will be and how this person has dealt with other abuse cases.[64] Bancroft writes that custody evaluators often lull you into a false feeling of security when they meet with you. You might think with a professional looking at your case your children will be more protected. This may or may not be true. Here is my story as an example.

My experience with a custody evaluator

Our custody evaluator came to my house to meet my children and me. She was a very sweet Christian woman, and I was made to believe she was my friend. This was a bad mistake on my part. I told her things about my insecurities as a mother, and I had not been a perfect wife.

These words came back to haunt me during the final orders of our divorce. Another error I made was not putting on a show for her. I allowed my kids to go about their business while I talked to her. I found out later my ex had engaged in a "rousing game of Boggle" with our kids when she visited his apartment. This led her to believe he was more of a "hands-on parent" than I was.

Later, I was told I should have treated the custody evaluator's visit like a house showing and pulled out all the stops! So my conclusion is: impress the heck out of the custody evaluator! Let them see your strengths as a parent. Also, anytime you speak to *anyone* from the court, less is more. Keep things close to the vest. Better for them to have to ask more questions than for you to divulge too much.

Bancroft recommends you have your lawyer with you anytime you speak to your custody evaluator. He says many evaluators will try to dissuade you from doing this, saying they just want to have a "friendly talk." Many lawyers are reluctant to attend because the evaluators sometimes get irritated. But he says the reason evaluators don't like having an attorney present is they know they will have to be much more professional about what they do and will not be able to intimidate or manipulate you.[65] If you have no lawyer, or decide not to include him/her when you meet with the evaluator, remember, your evaluator is *not* your friend. She is there to decide whether you can keep your children. This is serious. Plan out her visit as if the happiness of your children depends on it. Impress her with your housekeeping skills and the level of love and attention you give your children in her presence. Do not say anything negative about your ex (or your children) to her.

> Lundy Bancroft recommends you have your lawyer present whenever you speak to your custody evaluator.

Present any concerns you have about him in terms of concerns you have about your children. Also, remember to say "our children" instead of "my children." This will give the evaluator the impression you are willing to work with your ex in the best interest of your kids.

I know a counselor who has worked with custody evaluators who have been good advocates for the children in such cases. I pray that would be your experience.

Consider calling a domestic violence expert to speak in your custody case

Currently, judges in family court rely on custody evaluators who have little training in domestic violence. Adding testimony from a domestic violence advocate can help educate your judge.

> Domestic violence advocates are the only professionals with the training to be expert witnesses in custody cases where domestic violence is present.

A recent study[66] concluded that domestic violence advocates are the only professionals who have the training needed to recognize when domestic violence is present, which helps provide safety for both victims and their children. More and more domestic violence advocates are being trained to speak as expert witnesses in custody hearings.

Once the judge accepts the advocate as an expert witness, he or she can present evidence about the long-term harm children experience[67] when they witness domestic violence, and that the best ways to limit the damage and improve the situation are to:

1. Safeguard the child from future abuse by not giving the abusive parent unsupervised visitation.

2. Get the child exercise, psychological therapy, and give them anti-inflammatories (stress causes inflammation in the body, which can be overcome with anti-inflammatories). Because of these recommendations, the non-abusive parent should be the person assigned to make medical decisions for the child.

3. Allow the non-abusive, safe parent to give the child plenty of emotional support; therefore the safe parent should be awarded custody of the child.

What if you suspect your ex is sexually abusing your children?

This is every mother's worst nightmare. I can't imagine the pain this might cause you. Here are steps to take.

1. **Pray.** Ask God for His wisdom, peace, and protection for you and your children. Hang onto Him even harder now than ever before. He cares, and He is there for you.

2. **Don't panic.** Possibly what happened is more innocent than it first sounds. Don't jump to conclusions. Even if your child is being sex-

ually abused, if she realizes you are really upset, she may clam up and give you no more information. Why? Possibly:

- because her father has threatened her if she tells anyone
- she is afraid you are too fragile to handle news this bad
- she thinks you are angry with *her* because *she* did something wrong, or
- she is upset, and your fear or anger will upset her more.

3. **Try to involve a therapist who specializes in children and abuse.** Encourage the therapist to have a relationship with your ex. If she doesn't, and she later makes recommendations to the court in your favor, the court may ignore her recommendations as being biased. If or when she does write recommendations, ask her to be very matter-of-fact and not to give orders to the court. For example, it would be better for her to say, "The child appears to be upset after visiting her father," rather than "Visits to her father should be stopped immediately." Also, "The child has made reports—these reports seem natural, and not coerced—of physical boundary violations by the father" is better than, "The child is clearly being sexually abused."

4. **Investigate before involving Social Services.** Sometimes Social Services will be helpful, other times not. If you report that your ex has sexually abused your child, and they do not take protective measures against him, your judge may assume you were trying to alienate your children from their father. Try making an anonymous call to your local women's crisis center (but not from your own phone). The call should be anonymous because women's center employees are mandated reporters; in other words, if they know a child is being abused, they must, by law, report it. Ask them how Social Services in your specific district usually respond to these types of calls. If it seems a call to Social Services would help get your kids away from your sexually predative ex, you may want to try this.

> If you suspect your ex is sexually abusing your child:
>
> 1. Pray; hold onto God.
> 2. Don't panic.
> 3. Involve a therapist.
> 4. Investigate before calling Social Services.
> 5. Get support for you and your kids.

5. **Get support for you and your children.** Many women's crisis centers will offer support groups for you and your kids. Find one and go. Not only will talking about your problems help you, other people may help you with ideas for action.

6. **Consider raising other concerns about your ex.** Your judge may discount reports of abuse, but investigate other reports. For instance, does he abuse drugs, drive recklessly, or have any other criminal record? These things can make a difference.

Should You Go into Hiding with Your Children?

Have you considered taking your children and going into hiding? If so, you are not alone. I have worked with mothers who seriously considered "kidnapping" their children, leaving the state, changing their identity, and never returning. I sympathize with them, but I can't condone this, no matter how desperate things look. Why?

First, if you take your kids and leave, you will have to cut ties with everyone you know: family, friends, coworkers; perhaps all relationships. Doing this will isolate you and possibly make it difficult for you to get jobs in the future. Just as important, you will have to live looking over your shoulder, and there is a good chance your abuser or the police will find you. But most important, if you are found, you will probably be sent to jail, possibly for years, and your children will be forced to live full time with your abuser. You will no longer be there to help keep them safe.

> I don't recommend you go into hiding with your children because:
> 1. You will be isolated, losing all family and friends.
> 2. You may not be able to find work.
> 3. The police will probably find you.
> 4. If you are found, you will go to jail, and not be able to protect your kids.

So I can't recommend you take your kids and run. Even though things may look desperate, God has not abandoned you. With Him on your side, your situation could turn around completely by tomorrow, or . . . it may not. Either way, He is walking beside you, giving you strength to be the best mom you can be under difficult circumstances.

Summary

Seeking healing for your children who have experienced abuse is a difficult task, especially if they are still in contact with their abusive father. You may find your children, who behaved well when you lived with your abuser, have suddenly become belligerent, moody, throw tantrums, or cry excessively, all seemingly for no reason. They may even begin abusing you in the same way your ex used to.

All of this happens when you are still healing from the abuse you've experienced. You may be struggling with addictions, PTSD, depression, and/or low self-esteem. Focusing on your children's healing may seem an insurmountable task. You may feel as if this period in your lives will never end, and you may want to give up the fight—even to the point of willingly allowing your ex full custody of your children.

If you are in this spot, try to remember this is only one season of your life, a season that will pass in time. Think about all you have already overcome to get free of your abuser alive, with your soul still intact. He tried to take your mind, soul, strength, and possibly your life—but you resisted him and you are still here. You won that battle! You can win this battle as well. You are not alone. Jesus is walking beside you. He will never leave you, nor forsake you (Hebrews 13:5). You will have days when you will struggle to believe this because you won't *feel* his presence. On these days, you will need to trust Him and His Word. Surround yourself with people who will support you and hang on for the sake of your kids and your own healing.

Going to court against your abuser to fight for the custody of your children is one of the hardest things you may ever have to do. The family courts are now biased against female domestic violence survivors. The more you learn and prepare, the better your chances of winning at least half-time custody of your children. To learn more, I recommend Lundy Bancroft's book, *When Dad Hurts Mom*.[68]

A Drink of Water
for the Journey

Being a mother means that
your heart is no longer yours; it wanders
wherever your children do.

—AUTHOR UNKNOWN

1. Do your children show any signs that they have experienced fear from the abuse you have all experienced? If so, what are they?

2. What things can you do to rebuild your children's trust in you?

3. What things have you already done to help your children heal? What other suggestions would you like to try?

4. Do your children ever release their distressing feelings in startling ways? If so, how does this make you feel? How do you react?

5. Can you think of teachable moments you can find to help your kids learn to think critically?

6. Do your kids need safety planning? If so, should you do the planning with them or ask a domestic violence advocate, therapist, or someone else to provide this?

7. In what ways can you work with the court and your ex for the sake of your kids?

8. Have you ever used a custody evaluator? If so, describe your experience.

9. Have you ever suspected your ex of sexually molesting your children? If so, what did you do about it?

10. Have you ever considered going into hiding with your kids? Why? What would be the pros and cons of that choice?

CHAPTER 8

Forgive Your Abuser, Others—and Yourself

... release from darkness for the prisoners,
to proclaim the year of the Lord's favor
and the day of vengeance of our God ...

—ISAIAH 61:1, 2

Forgiving an abuser may seem to be an impossible task. Perhaps even the mention of it makes you angry. You may think I'm crazy or heartless to even suggest you should forgive your abuser. Yet I believe learning to forgive him is one of the most important things you can do for yourself as you journey toward healing.

Often, Christians will press abuse victims to "forgive" their abusers, when what they really want is for the victim to reconcile with her abuser. They are in essence asking the victim to ignore the sins the abuser has perpetrated upon her, allowing the abuser to continue abusing her. This helps no one. The abuser is not held accountable for his actions and given the chance to repent; therefore, he continues his abuse. The victim continues in her role as victim—helpless and without a voice. She is not freed from her justifiable anger and does not have a chance to heal. Even the church as a whole is harmed, because it doesn't become a place

> The forgiveness described in this chapter is not about reconciling with your abuser, but about letting go of the bitterness you hold toward him that is harming *you.*

of healing but remains a place where abuse is tolerated and lies, rather than truth, exist. As a result, many abuse victims leave the church and turn their backs on God.

If you have experienced this, I can only imagine the pain and anger you must feel. The type of forgiveness I describe in this chapter has nothing to do with reconciling with your abuser. It has more to do with letting go of bitterness and anger toward him that is harming *you*. I hope you will read on to try to understand why I believe forgiving your abuser and others who have hurt you is so important.

My Experience with Forgiveness

Like many abused women, I struggled with forgiveness, and sometimes still do. I had to forgive my ex-husband for years of abuse. I needed to forgive a marriage counselor we had gone to for ways he failed to keep me safe. I also had to forgive two pastors in my church that I'd gone to for help during the last years of my awful marriage. Not only did they not help me, but when I finally got a restraining order and kicked my husband out, they told me I had "no right" to divorce. Finally, I had to forgive many people who worked in the family court system.

My biggest challenge with forgiveness came after my divorce. When I divorced my abusive husband I was very naïve about the family court system. I assumed the court system would want to keep my children away from their abusive father. I was wrong. The custody evaluator we hired to protect our children decided early on it was "best for the children" if they spent one week with me and the entire next week with my abusive soon-to-be ex-husband. I was shocked, appalled, and angry, but I had no choice but to accept her decision. When it came time for final orders, my lawyer suggested I petition the court to extend my temporary civil restraining order to a permanent restraining order to keep myself safe. She also suggested I petition the court to have full decision-making rights for the children, since negotiating with my abusive husband was impossible. He did whatever he wanted and I had no say in the matter. I was sure he would make decisions for the children, simply to hurt me, that would not be in their best interest.

In order to prove my need for these things, our judge allowed my husband's lawyer to question me on the witness stand for eight grueling hours. The next day, when it was my lawyer's turn to question my husband, his lawyer objected to every question, and the judge sustained each objection. In other words, from my perspective, my husband didn't have to answer any questions, and I was treated like a criminal. The judge denied both my petitions. I was not allowed to keep my restraining order, so I had no physical protection from him, and we were to have joint decision-making custody of the children.

I was so angry I stayed up all night screaming and crying. This was very unusual behavior for me. When the sun finally came up, I called my counselor for an emergency appointment. I didn't think anything could make me feel better, but she shared these truths that helped me:

- Even though the judge and the custody evaluator didn't believe you had been abused, you know the truth, and God knows the truth.

- You are not the same person you were when you were still married. He is still an abuser, but you are no longer a battered woman. You are much stronger than you used to be.

- He no longer has any control over you. He used to control your actions, thoughts, prayers, finances, and children in order to make you feel weak and helpless. He no longer has control in those areas, except for your children, but only half the time. Further, *he knows* he no longer has control over you. He knows you will not remain silent if he abuses you. He knows people are watching him, including the police if he becomes physically dangerous.

- You are finally divorced and free of him, and you can live your life the way you want. You no longer take or need input from him.

I asked my counselor how to get rid of the burning anger I was feeling, which was making me physically ill. She told me three very important things: I had every right to be angry at first (this is quite normal); I needed to realize my anger was springing from my hurt and that I further needed to find what is causing the hurt; and third, I should go ahead and feel anger initially. The key, she said, was to not allow bitterness to overtake me.

Regarding finding the source of my hurt, I tried to discern what was so painful. I decided it was the fact I had been grilled for eight hours and had poured out my heart, telling them what my husband had put me through, and the judge basically said, "I don't care."

I then asked my counselor how to forgive those who had hurt me.

She said the way to do this is to have compassion. For example, I can have compassion for the custody evaluator because she must have a difficult job dealing with two parents who see things from completely different viewpoints, and the children, who each have their own needs as well. This would not be an enjoyable job. I can have compassion for my ex-husband's attorney because he had to interact with and defend an abuser—what a miserable job! And these things did help me, though I felt as if my heart was still broken.

And this is how God works: I was not at all surprised the next Sunday when my pastor preached on forgiveness! The main points of the sermon were that extending forgiveness to one who has hurt you is probably the most difficult thing for a Christian (or anyone) to do, and that we need to forgive without limits (Jesus said "seventy times seven"). In Matthew 6:14, 15, Jesus said that if we will not forgive others, God will not forgive our sins.

The pastor made the further points that even though we are called to forgive, this doesn't mean we should allow the person to continue abusing us, especially in cases of spouse or child abuse. Also, we need to allow the abuser to feel the consequences of his behavior, whether it is time in jail, going to a class for abusers, losing his home and family, his position in the church, or a combination of or all of these things. He used Matthew 18:27 as a definition of forgiveness: the servant's master took pity on him, canceled the debt, and let him go.

Both of these people were using Jesus' words to show me that I need to take pity on—or have compassion for—the other person. To forgive and love our enemies is not something we can do on our own—at all! We have to forgive and love with the love and forgiveness of Jesus. Jesus has forgiven every sin we've ever committed, and every sin we will ever commit. Because we've been forgiven much, we need to forgive others. And it's important that we understand we are never more like God than when we forgive others who have sinned against us.

All of this was reinforced in that sermon. After hearing it, I decided I needed to get serious about learning to forgive. My journey toward forgiveness has been a long one, but the Lord has walked me through it. I knew this project would take some major time, so I spent an entire day at Christian retreat center near my home. They have a free room you can reserve for the day to be used for prayer. I brought my journals, the

Bible, and many books on forgiveness. I went through my journals to reread what I was forgiving people for. I didn't want this to be a surface forgiveness, but real, gut-wrenching forgiveness.

I started with trying to forgive the people I thought would be easier to forgive, like the pastor at my church. I believed he had handled my situation badly but had sincerely done what he thought was best. Next I moved to the lawyers and officers of the court. Even before I tried to forgive my ex-husband, forgiving others freed my heart to be at peace with him to some degree. My counselor told me that while she was impressed with my willingness to forgive, it might take some time. She told me that in a year, the pain wouldn't be as fresh, and it would be easier—and she was right.

Over the next few months, I spent several days at the retreat center and eventually tackled the difficult job of forgiving my husband. Again, I took my journals with me in order to remember the abusive things he had done to me. As I prayed over each one, I felt the Lord's peace come into my heart. I learned that deciding to forgive him was a decision I made, an "event," but actually forgiving him was—and still is— an ongoing process. There are days, even now, years later, when I remember something he did to me that I had buried in the back of my mind, and anger rises up inside of me. When this happens, I turn it over to the Lord anew. The Lord has held my hand through this process, just like every other step along the difficult path of my life. As He promised in Hebrews 13:5:

> Deciding to forgive someone is an event, but actually forgiving is an ongoing process.

"Never will I leave you; never will I forsake you."

Misconceptions About Forgiveness

Forgiving your abuser is hard. Perhaps thinking about it is making your blood boil. Often, people have misconceptions about forgiveness that make it harder for them to forgive. So I'd like to dispense with four misconceptions you may have about forgiveness.

Misconception #1: If you forgive your abuser, you must reconcile with him.

This is not true. Forgiving him has nothing to do with reconciliation. If you have reconciled with your abuser, forgiving him will be important, since you will need to forgive him in order to continue living with him. But even if you haven't reconciled, and you feel what he did to you is unforgiveable, please read on.

Misconception #2: You can or should only forgive him if he admits he was wrong. Perhaps you have decided not to forgive your abuser until he acknowledges the wrongs he's committed against you and asks for your forgiveness. If so, please be aware there is very little chance this will happen. Why not? He may honestly believe he has done nothing wrong, and/or he may be too prideful to admit he ever wronged you. Waiting for this will prevent you from being able to forgive him.

Misconception #3: You haven't really forgiven him unless you have forgotten what he has done to you.

As Christians, we often hear the phrase "forgive and forget." Did you know this phrase does not appear in the Bible? You can search for it, but you will never find it. Jesus tells us to forgive in Luke 17:1-4, but He never tells us to forget. Instead, *forgive* and *remember* what you have learned from your experience. This will prevent you from getting into another abusive relationship in the future, and will allow you to help others who are going through abuse. You will move into a new future free of anger and bitterness.

> Four misconceptions about forgiveness:
> - If you forgive your abuser, you must reconcile with him
> - You can only forgive him if he admits he was wrong
> - You must forget what he has done to you
> - You forgive him for his benefit

Misconception #4: You forgive him for his benefit.

This is also not true. You forgive him to help *you*, not him. I have learned forgiveness sometimes blesses others, but mostly blesses me. Often, the person I am angry with isn't aware of my anger, or doesn't care! When I hold on to anger and grudges, they are like a cancer inside me, one that can consume me. It does me more harm than the other person.

Why Should You Forgive Your Abuser?

Once these four misconceptions are out of the way, learning to forgive is an easier process. I can now ask the question: *Why should I forgive him?* I see two principal reasons.

> Forgive your abuser so that:
> • you are no longer tied to him
> • you don't become bitter and defile others

So You Are No Longer Tied to Him!

To forgive your abuser means to let him off the hook or cancel the debt he owes you. When you refuse to forgive him, you still want something from him, even if it is revenge or a confession of what he did.

Wanting something from him keeps you tied to him forever.

You may have struggled for months or even years to leave your abuser. Now you've taken back your life. If you refuse to forgive him, he still owns a part of you, and you will never be free. Do you want him to have that power?

So You Don't Become Bitter and Defile Others

In the pamphlet *Forgiveness, Healing the Harbored Hurts of Your Heart*, Bill Elliff and Tim Grissom describe another good reason to forgive. They explain that no matter what your initial reactions to pain might be, you only have two ways to deal with your hurt. You can either harbor the hurt and become bitter, or heal the hurt God's way.[69]

What does harboring the hurt mean? When seas get rough, ships look for a harbor. A harbor is a body of water near a coast where a ship can anchor safely. When we are hurt, we often look for a place to anchor or save the hurt in our heart . . . unaware that hurt has a life of its own.

Elliff and Grissom write:

> In reality, the smallest particle of harbored hurt carries deadly potency, just as one cancer cell has the potential to [kill] the strongest of men. Would you be content to do nothing if you knew that just a few cancer cells had been found in your body? Are you also willing to look with indifference to the hurts of your heart? If Satan can keep you blinded to the presence of bitterness, however small and harmless it may seem, he has an open door.[70]

Once the hurt is tucked away in your heart, a root of bitterness can grow in your soul. After it is there, it can hurt you in ways you are unaware of. It can rob you of your joy and peace. Then it may subtly distance you from God. How can you have sweet fellowship with God when you are holding a grudge against someone? You can't. It will interrupt your prayers and take over your thought life.

Next, it turns you into a person you don't want to be. Have you ever met a bitter woman? If you ask her, would she say she is bitter? Probably not. Yet this is clear to all who are around her. And does her bitterness diminish over the years? No, it actually grows. She is more bitter at age 75 than she was when she was hurt at 35.

And sadly, she most likely has infected others with her bitterness. Like an infectious disease, her bitterness is catching. She has "passed it" to her friends and family and especially her children. Sometimes her children are even more bitter than their mother ever was, and their children even more bitter still. Her grandchildren don't even know why they are bitter. This is what Hebrews 12:15 means about defiling many: *See to it that no one falls short of the grace of God and that no bitter root grows up to cause trouble and defile many.*

Are you willing to defile *anyone* you know and love in order to hold onto and harbor the hurt in your heart by being unwilling to forgive?

Learning How to Forgive the Unforgiveable

Have you decided you don't want to defile anyone else through holding onto your bitterness toward your abuser? If so, how do you learn to forgive? In the pamphlet *Forgiveness*, Elliff and Grissom provide six steps, advice I used to forgive my ex-husband. I have added a seventh step, from Steven R. Tracy, because I believe it is so crucial. I hope you find these steps as helpful as I did.[71]

1. Recognize and admit your own sin.

This is a really tough one! You might be thinking, *WHAT? Why should I admit my sin? I'm the victim here! He's the one who abused me!* You're right, but we aren't talking about him. You are the one who needs to be freed from bitterness and learn to forgive. So ask

> Though you are the victim of abuse, in order to be free, you must first confess sins you've committed along the way.

yourself: are you hoping to get back at him somehow? In Romans 12:17, Paul says: *Do not repay anyone evil for evil.*

Have you slandered him? Have you been harsh with your children because of his abuse? I found I couldn't forgive my husband until I confessed the sins I had committed because my conscience wouldn't release me! That is why this is the first in a long line of difficult steps.

2. Accept that God allowed this painful experience in your life for a reason you may never understand.

In Romans 8:28, Paul writes:

> *And we know that in all things God works for the good of those who love him, who have been called according to his purpose.*

Does this mean everything that happens to a Christian will be good? Hardly. In fact, a few verses later, in Romans 8:35, Paul talks about some of the things that happened to him:

> *. . . trouble or hardship or persecution or famine or nakedness or danger or sword . . .*

We certainly wouldn't call these things good. Yet God can work things for your good even in the midst of things like these, even in the midst of abuse—if you allow Him to. God may allow you to see something beautiful coming from your pain, such as growing closer to Him, learning empathy for others, or having the opportunity to help other abuse victims. And it is possible that you may never see anything beautiful coming from it in this life. You may never understand why He allowed the abuse to happen to you. This is a hard truth, and you will have to trust that God has a bigger plan for your life and your pain than you can imagine. Accepting this hard truth will help you release your anger and bitterness over it.

> God may have a purpose for your abuse and pain that you may never know or understand. Learning to accept this will help you forgive your abuser.

3. Forgive: release the debt.

At this point, you most likely will not feel like forgiving your abuser; forgiveness will be more an act of your will. In 1 Corinthians 13:5, Paul says that love *keeps no record of wrongs.*

The phrase "keeping a record" brings to mind a storekeeper who has a ledger on which he keeps a list of what each customer owes him. He keeps these records because he plans to collect a payment in the future. You may have a ledger in your heart where you have listed every wrong your abuser has committed against you. If so, you may think, *He owes me, and I'm going to make him pay.*

> At this point you probably won't feel like forgiving your abuser; it will be an act of your will.

But God says, in Romans 12:19:

Do not take revenge, my dear friends, but leave room for God's wrath, for it is written: "It is mine to avenge; I will repay," says the Lord.

Elliff writes, "When I was tempted to seek revenge from a person who had wronged me, a friend once told me, 'Bill, God only allows two people at a time in the boxing ring. If you want to get into the ring and try to fight your own battles, God will let you, but He'll get out. If you want God to fight your battles for you, then you must get out of the ring . . . and stay out.'"[72]

Allowing God to avenge the wrong your abuser has caused you will take an act of faith on your part. You will need to trust Him. As Psalm 9:9, 10 says:

The Lord is a refuge for the oppressed, a stronghold in times of trouble.

Those who know your name trust in you, for you, Lord, have never forsaken those who seek you.

What if the person you're angry and bitter toward is God Himself? After all, He is powerful, and while He didn't cause your abuse, He *did* allow it. Don't try to hide your anger from Him. He already knows about it! Be honest with Him. Scream, weep, and wail. King David did these very things! Then ask Him to free you from your bitterness toward Him.

4. Ask God to exchange His love for your hatred.

At this moment, you may be filled with hatred for your abuser. It may be hard to imagine loving him with God's unconditional, unselfish love. Yet, in Matthew 5:38-48, Jesus calls us to love our enemies. This is impossible if God is not involved. If you have a genuine relationship with

God through faith in Jesus, the Holy Spirit resides in you, and God can miraculously pour out His love in your heart.

And hope does not put us to shame, because God's love has been poured out into our hearts through the Holy Spirit, who has been given to us (Romans 5:5).

In his book, *Mending the Soul*, Steven R. Tracy gives a practical idea for how to do this.[73] He states that abuse victims tend to see their abusers only as the sum of all the abusive acts they have committed. Of course, it's true that the abuse may be the most important thing about your abuser to you, and in no way should be minimized. However, his abusive actions are not the only thing about his humanity. He is a human being, just as you are. He was once a newborn baby, and once a small child. Many (but not all) abusers were also abused or neglected as children. Every abuser is a human being created in God's image, a person who has been manipulated by Satan into doing harmful actions to attempt to meet their needs, and to cope with their pain in inappropriate, sinful ways. If you can look at your abuser through the eyes of compassion, you may find it easier to begin to love him with God's love.

5. Pray about your abuse—with thanksgiving.

In 1 Thessalonians, 5:16-18 Paul writes:

Rejoice always, pray continually, give thanks in all circumstances; for this is God's will for you in Christ Jesus.

I know this sounds like a crazy thing to say. Why would anyone ask you to rejoice right now, to thank God for allowing you to be abused? How could God ask that of you? As always, He doesn't ask you to do this on your own. He is alongside you, holding your hand. Philippians 4:4-8 is my favorite passage of the Bible because I tend to be an anxious person:

Rejoice in the Lord always. I will say it again: Rejoice!
Let your gentleness be evident to all. The Lord is near.
Do not be anxious about anything, but in every situation,
by prayer and petition, with thanksgiving, present your requests to God.
And the peace of God, which transcends all understanding,
will guard your hearts and your minds in Christ Jesus.

Finally, brothers and sisters, whatever is true, whatever is noble, whatever is right, whatever is pure, whatever is lovely, whatever is admirable—if anything is excellent or praiseworthy—think about such things.

Paul implores me to "rejoice . . . always" and to let my "gentleness be evident to all." Gentleness is not the first adjective people use to describe me when I am anxious about something, but Paul tells me how I can become less anxious. He exhorts me to remember that "the Lord is near," and to pray about *every* situation with thanksgiving. This made no sense to me for many

> Giving God a sacrifice of praise will help bring you peace in your pain.

years. Recently, a friend helped me. She looks for *any* little thing she can be thankful for in a situation, and she praises God for these things when she is anxious. She calls this a sacrifice of praise (Hebrews 13:15). Often it is a sacrifice to praise God when we don't feel like it!

Here's an example of how I pray about my abuse with praise: "Lord, you know how much pain I experienced at the hand of my ex-husband. Please help me get past that pain and help me begin to heal. Also, please help my children begin to heal as well. Lord, though I don't feel thankful to have experienced this, I choose to offer you a sacrifice of praise. I thank you for walking through those hard years with me. You never left me, nor did you forsake me. I may never have come to believe in your Son as my savior if my marriage had been easy, Lord, so I thank you for the difficulties that drew me closer to you. I thank you that because I became a Christian, my children are now Christians as well. And even though they had to experience much pain at the hands of their father because of mistakes I made, and because of our divorce, you drew them closer to you through their pain. Thank you for allowing me to write *A Journey through Emotional Abuse: From Bondage to Freedom*, as well as this book. I pray these two books will be a blessing to many women. Please Lord, bring them freedom and peace. Please continue to walk with me in the days ahead, and point me in the direction you would have me walk. Amen."

When you pray with thanksgiving, God's peace will guard your heart and mind (Philippians 4:7). This is a gift that goes beyond our ability to understand.

6. Extend appropriate grace.

In his book, Steven Tracy takes forgiveness one step further. He encourages abuse victims to not only give up their desire to hate and even seek revenge, but to have an inner desire for good things for their abuser.[74] This goes along with Jesus's mandate to love our enemies (Matthew 5:43-48). Again, this does not mean you must reconcile with him. But it does mean you could begin praying God's best for him, which might include:

> You can extend grace to your abuser by praying he will repent of his distorted beliefs that allow him to abuse others.

- he would be stripped of his distorted beliefs that allow him to think it is OK to abuse others

- he would repent and turn from his abusive ways

- he would receive God's forgiveness and find his own healing.

This step might seem nearly impossible, but wouldn't it be wonderful if your abuser would repent and stop abusing you and others?

7. Continually and instantly keep forgiving.

Deciding to forgive your abuser is an event. Forgiving him is a process that may take you a long time. You may completely forgive him; still, one day a memory of what he has done to you will return, and your anger and bitterness will come rushing back. At that point, you will have to forgive him again. Be patient with yourself, but don't allow Satan to gain a foothold in your heart by catching you unaware and reviving your feelings of anger and revenge. Each time this occurs, turn again to Jesus, and ask him to walk you through the steps listed here. 1 Thessalonians 5:24 says: *The one who calls you is faithful, and he will do it.*

> You may need to forgive your abuser many times. Be patient with yourself, and don't allow unforgiveness to creep back into your life.

Learning to Give Yourself the Grace of Forgiveness

If we confess our sins, he is faithful and just and will forgive us our sins and purify us from all unrighteousness (1 John 1:9).

As difficult as it is to forgive your abuser and others who have hurt you, you may find it even harder to forgive yourself. Why is this more difficult? If someone else hurts you, you can ignore or get away from that person. But you can't escape yourself. When you wake in the morning, you are still there. When you go to sleep at night: still there. Here are some reasons you might need to forgive yourself:

- for starting a relationship with your abuser
- for all the wasted time spent with him
- for the ways you allowed him to treat you
- for the way you acted and the things you did while you were with him
- for not protecting your child(ren)
- for getting a divorce/leaving him
- for "not being good enough" for him.

I can't list every reason you might feel guilty and need to forgive yourself. Your reasons may not make logical sense, even to you, such as "not being good enough" for him. Possibly, you don't feel you need to forgive yourself. If that's true, great!

Why Is Forgiving Yourself Important for Your Healing?

Perhaps you aren't sure going through the pain of forgiving yourself is worth the benefit. Here are some critical reasons.

To improve your health

Holding onto self-condemnation elevates your stress. Long-term chronic stress can cause depression and anxiety. In addition, it can cause a long list of physical ailments, including:[75]

- skin and hair problems, such as acne, psoriasis, eczema, and permanent hair loss
- menstrual problems, and an inability to conceive children
- sexual dysfunction (impotence, premature ejaculation in men, loss of sexual desire in both men and women)
- eating disorders and obesity

- gastrointestinal problems (heartburn, gastritis, ulcerative colitis, irritable colon)

- high blood pressure, abnormal heart rhythms, increased risk of heart disease, heart attacks, and stroke

- sleep problems, fatigue, exhaustion

- ongoing pain, joint pain, headaches, backaches.

> **Forgiving yourself will help:**
>
> - Improve your health
> - Bring you peace
> - Enable you to focus on others
> - Repair your relationship with God

To bring you peace

Guilt and self-blame weigh you down. You may hear a constant negative voice in your head reminding you of all the supposedly unforgivable wrongs you've committed. Whether that voice is Satan's, your abuser's, a parent's, or your own, it doesn't really matter. You will never be at peace with those negative thoughts constantly circling through your head. Forgiving yourself will release you to be at peace.

To enable you to focus on others

When you are focused on your own guilt, you have little emotional energy to give to others around you. Forgiving yourself releases you to be able to love others as you've loved yourself (Mark 12:29-31).

To repair your relationship with God

When you cannot forgive yourself, you may mistakenly believe God cannot forgive you. This may cause you to pull away from Him, or constantly beg His forgiveness, when He has already forgiven you completely (Psalm 103:12, Hebrews 10:17, 1 John 1:9). Once you forgive yourself, your relationship with God can be fully repaired.

What Are the Steps to Forgiving Yourself?

Step 1: Seek God's forgiveness

God is a God of forgiveness. Giving everyone in the world an opportunity for forgiveness was why Jesus came to earth (John 3:16)! God knows every sin we've ever committed. We can't hide them from Him anymore than we can hide them from ourselves. 1 John 1:8-10 says:

If we claim to be without sin, we deceive ourselves and the truth is not in us. If we confess our sins, He is faithful and just and will forgive us our sins and purify us from all unrighteousness. If we claim we have not sinned, we make Him out to be a liar and His word is not in us.

Besides God's knowledge of our sins, He is the only one who can give us the strength to forgive ourselves. Therefore, going to Him is the first step in forgiving ourselves.

Forgive Yourself, Step 1: Humbly ask God to forgive you for the wrongs you have committed.

When you ask God's forgiveness, you must be honest about what you have done. Have you ever had a child say "I'm sorry" because they knew you expected it, but you knew they weren't sorry? God also can tell when we aren't sorry. When we fully accept the blame for our sin, and humbly ask His forgiveness, He is faithful and just to forgive our sins.

You must also repent of that sin. To repent means you will turn 180 degrees in the opposite direction of the sin. It does no good to say "I'm sorry" for a sin you plan to repeat tomorrow. Repentance means you fully expect and plan to never repeat that sin again. You will ask for God's help, knowing you cannot do this on your own.

Lastly, you must take responsibility for your sins. You will never be able to truly forgive yourself for your sins if you don't take responsibility for committing them. If you just let yourself "off the hook," and make excuses for what you've done, or try to forget your actions, your conscience will not allow you to forget the offense. It will bring your offense to mind again and again until you humble yourself and admit the wrong you've committed and make an effort to make it right. Taking responsibility for your sins leads to the second step.

Step 2: Make restitution

What does making restitution mean? Webster's dictionary defines it as:

- the act of returning something that was lost or stolen to its owner

- payment that is made to someone for damage, trouble, etc.[76]

In other words, restitution is attempting to fix something you've broken by taking the proper actions.

As a former abuse victim, I can say that understanding how to make restitution can be tricky, depending on what you are trying to forgive yourself for. For example, you may feel guilty for behaving poorly toward your abuser, believing your actions may have been part of the reason he abused you. Apologizing and making things right with him may bring you back into relationship with him—and put yourself back in danger—which would not be wise. You may feel guilty for wasting years of your life with him. In this case, you cannot go back and re-live the years you wasted, but you can decide to make the best of your future years. On the other hand, if you feel guilty for putting your children in harm's way by staying with your abuser too long, you can make restitution with them. Hence, deciding how to make restitution may require you to think creatively.

> **Forgive Yourself, Step 2:** Making restitution can be tricky for abuse victims. Deciding how may require you to think creatively.

To make restitution with a person other than your abuser (i.e., someone who is safe for you to have regular contact with), you need to see how your action has hurt them from their perspective. When you do this, you must realize they may see the pain you caused them as more grievous than you do. You will first want to apologize, saying, "Yes, I did do that," without excusing your actions by saying, "But you also hurt me," or, "Yes, I did that, but I was not feeling well," or, "Yes, I did that, but I really had no choice." Try to simply own what you did, leaving off the "but." Say, "Yes, I did that, and I'm sorry for how it hurt you." For example, you might say to your children, "I am sorry for all the pain I caused you by staying with my abuser for so long. I can only imagine all the ways living in a house with so much fear has hurt you through the years." You won't help your kids if you then add, "But you will never realize how hard I tried to shield you from some of his abuse."

Don't expect your kids to instantly forgive you. The hurt they've experienced cannot be forgiven instantly. Be prepared to apologize more than once. Also, be prepared to *do* something to make amends for the hurt you've caused them. What are some ways you can do this?

- Get them counseling to help with their healing.

- Become—and remain—strong yourself.

- Find a good job and/or get some education so you can provide for them.

- Help find them some good role models.

Your children may not forgive you for many years. You can't control this. You don't need to wait many years to forgive yourself, however. Apologize, then begin performing actions that will help them—and begin forgiving yourself.

Step 3: Make a decision to consciously forgive yourself

After you have asked God to forgive you, and done whatever you could to make things right with others, you will need to make a conscious decision to forgive yourself. At this point, you may not feel forgiving toward yourself, but at some point you will need to decide to do so. In their book, *The Meaning of Marriage: Facing the Complexities of Commitment with the Wisdom of God*, Timothy and Kathy Keller describe the gospel this way: "We are more sinful and flawed in ourselves than we ever dared believe, yet at the very same time we are more loved and accepted in Jesus Christ than we ever dared hope."[77]

> Forgive Yourself, Step 3: Decide to forgive yourself. As Timothy and Kathy Keller say, "We are more sinful than we dare believe, and more loved in Jesus than we dare hope."

Accepting that you are a flawed, sinful person might seem counterproductive. Aren't we trying to help you forgive yourself? But you must grasp this: you are more sinful than you are aware. At the same time, guess what? So am I. So are your mom, your best friend, your boss, your child, and your neighbor. We all spend a lot of time and energy hiding this fact from each other. You don't need to hide it from yourself or from God. Once you accept the magnitude of your sinfulness, you can begin accepting the amazing, joyous fact that God loves you more than you will ever imagine. Ephesians 3:17-19 says:

> *And I pray that you, being rooted and established in love, may have power, together with all the Lord's holy people, to grasp how wide and long and high and deep is the love of Christ, and to know this love that surpasses knowledge—that you may be filled to the measure of all the fullness of God.*

Sometimes the Bible becomes mere words to us. Try to really feel how much God loves you. Put it in real terms. Pick someone you love more than anyone else in the world. If you have a child, he or she will be a good choice. If not, choose a sibling or parent. Now picture in your mind another person you love. Let's say the only way that second person could live is if your loved one dies a horrible, humiliating, painful death. Could you sacrifice your favorite person for that second person? That is what God did for you. He loved you enough to sacrifice His Son, His only Son, to come to earth, suffer, and die a painful, humiliating death.

> Would you be willing to sacrifice your favorite person so another person could live? God did this for you. *This is the gospel.*

You may think God didn't do that specifically for you. Yes, He did. Accept this. This is the extent of His love for you. If you haven't accepted this sacrifice Jesus made for you, now is the time to do it. Pray to God. Ask Him to forgive you. Tell Jesus you want Him to be your savior. You will be amazed how joyous you will feel and how transformed your life will be.

If you have just accepted Jesus' sacrifice for you, I urge you to tell someone right away. You probably know a Christian who has been praying for you. Call that person immediately! If not, you can call K-LOVE, a Christian radio station[78] that has pastors on call 24 hours a day. They will help you find a church close to you that will help you grow in your faith and relationship with the Lord. Forgive yourself. Now is the time. Make the decision; your feelings will catch up.

Step 4: Challenge negative self-talk

Once you have sought God's forgiveness, made restitution with others, and decided to forgive yourself, you may find you still focus on your past sins: all the ways you have hurt others or let yourself down. Perhaps you do so even to an obsessive level. You may not realize you constantly rehash your shortcomings throughout each day. It's like a broken record that plays over and over in your mind. You won't be at peace with yourself until you break this pattern of negative self-talk.

Journal Your Journey

In Chapter 3, I described how to break the habit of negative self-talk. Write down every automatic thought you have for a week. Once you see what you are saying to yourself, you can turn those negative thoughts into positive ones. For example:

Negative thoughts	Positive thoughts
I am a terrible person.	I am loved by God.
No one will ever forgive me.	God has forgiven me.
I never do anything good.	I have done/am doing all I can to make amends for the wrongs I've done.

Whenever you hear yourself speaking negatively, purposely exchange the negative sentence for the positive one.

Cognitive-behavioral therapy, which I describe in Chapter 6, can also help turn around negative automatic thoughts. Try questioning your thoughts. Ask yourself, "Am I being a perfectionist? Am I holding myself to a higher standard than I would someone else? What would a friend say about this? What would I tell a friend if they were struggling with this? How long should I suffer for this sin?" If you find you cannot break out of your negative self-talk, consider seeking a CBT therapist.

> **Forgive Yourself, Step 4:** Challenge your negative self-talk:
>
> • Turn negative thoughts into positive ones
> • Question your negative thoughts
> • Use cognitive-behavioral therapy
> • Fight a spiritual battle with spiritual weapons

Finally, consider the possibility that you may be fighting a spiritual battle. Jesus came to set us free (John 8:36, Romans 8:1-4, Galatians 5:1), but Satan works against Jesus' purposes for our lives. If you continue to struggle with self-blame, you might be trapped in a spiritual stronghold. Satan would love for you to remain mired in guilt and pain so you cannot live freely.

For though we live in the world, we do not wage war as the world does. The weapons we fight with are not the weapons of the world. On the contrary, they have divine power to demolish strongholds. We demolish arguments and every pretension that sets itself up against the knowledge of God, and we take captive every thought to make it obedient to Christ (2 Corinthians 10:3-5).

Paul suggests taking every thought captive and making it obedient to Christ. Christ came to set us free, even free from our own self-condemnation. Which weapons "not of the world" is Paul talking about?

Finally, be strong in the Lord and in his mighty power. Put on the full armor of God, so that you can take your stand against the devil's schemes. For our struggle is not against flesh and blood, but against the rulers, against the authorities, against the powers of this dark world and against the spiritual forces of evil in the heavenly realms. Therefore put on the full armor of God, so that when the day of evil comes, you may be able to stand your ground, and after you have done everything, to stand. Stand firm then, with the belt of truth buckled around your waist, with the breastplate of righteousness in place, and with your feet fitted with the readiness that comes from the gospel of peace. In addition to all this, take up the shield of faith, with which you can extinguish all the flaming arrows of the evil one. Take the helmet of salvation and the sword of the Spirit, which is the word of God.

And pray in the Spirit on all occasions with all kinds of prayers and requests. With this in mind, be alert and always keep on praying for all the Lord's people (Ephesians 6:10-18).

The weapons:

God's truth: believers are loved and forgiven.

Breastplate of righteousness: we don't have to be perfect; we are saved because of Jesus' perfection.

Gospel of peace: believers are saved, and become one with God. He loves us more than we can ever know. He is committed to us, and is fighting for us.

Shield of faith: our faith doesn't depend on our own strength. Our faith never fails because we've placed our faith in Jesus, and He never fails.

Helmet of salvation: our hope of salvation when we die gives us confidence that our present struggle with Satan will not last forever. We know we will be victorious in the end.

Sword of the Spirit, God's Word: the Bible, which transforms us, and brings us closer to him. Every word in the Bible was written in the power of the Holy Spirit (2 Timothy 3:16). They are God's words.

Be aware you should not fight a spiritual battle alone. No soldier goes into battle by himself. Ask fellow Christians to pray with you and help you in your battle against Satan. For more about spiritual warfare, I recommend Neil Anderson's book *The Bondage Breaker: Overcoming Negative Thoughts, Irrational Feelings, Habitual Sins.*[79]

Step 5: Return to the steps used to forgive others listed earlier in this chapter

The steps I outlined earlier about forgiving others can be used to solidify your self-forgiveness process. Reread them if it will help. Briefly, the steps are:

1. Recognize and admit your own sin.

2. Accept that God allowed this painful experience in your life for a reason you may never understand in this life.

3. Forgive: remind yourself you have already been forgiven. You are more flawed than you ever believed, but more loved than you can possibly imagine.

4. Ask God to exchange His love for your hatred—especially if you wrestle with a self-hatred or self-disgust.

> Forgive Yourself, Step 5: Return to the steps used to forgive others listed earlier in this chapter.

5. Pray—with thanksgiving—about your experience.

6. Pray that you may receive grace from God.

7. Continually and instantly keep forgiving.
   Like any hard-won battle, forgiving yourself is not something you do once and are finished.

＊ ＊ ＊ ＊ ＊

Many people in the church no longer listen to old hymns. The following hymn, written by Charitie L. Bancroft in 1863, is hauntingly beautiful. Whenever I am feeling ashamed, or am having trouble forgiving myself, I find peace in this hymn.

Before the Throne of God Above[80]

Before the Throne of God Above
I have a strong and perfect plea.
A great high Priest whose Name is Love
Who ever lives and pleads for me.

My name is graven on His hands,
My name is written on His heart.
I know that while in Heaven He stands
No tongue can bid me thence depart.
No tongue can bid me thence depart.
When Satan tempts me to despair
And tells me of the guilt within,
Upward I look and see Him there
Who made an end of all my sin.
Because the sinless Savior died
My sinful soul is counted free.
For God the just is satisfied
To look on Him and pardon me.
To look on Him and pardon me.
Behold Him there the risen Lamb,
My perfect spotless righteousness,
The great unchangeable I AM,
The King of glory and of grace,
One in Himself I cannot die.
My soul is purchased by His blood,
My life is hid with Christ on high,
With Christ my Savior and my God!
With Christ my Savior and my God!

Summary

Trust me when I tell you I know how hard it is to forgive your abuser. When I quote Bible verses I am not making light of how difficult this process is. Everything in us fights against forgiving those who hurt us, especially if they never admit what they've done wrong, and never apologize for it. You may dig in your heels and decide: *No, I won't do it!* That is, of course, your choice. However, I strongly believe this will hurt you more than it will ever hurt your abuser. You will pay the price for your decision in your level of peace and contentment, your relationships with others, and your physical health. I hope you will consider the cost and begin walking this difficult journey to forgiveness.

Besides forgiving your abuser, there may be many others who have hurt you along the way. You may even be having trouble forgiving your-self! God will bless you as you work toward forgiving yourself and others.

A Drink of Water for the Journey

Bless those who persecute you; bless and do not curse . . . Do not repay anyone evil for evil. Be careful to do what is right in the eyes of everyone. If it is possible, as far as it depends on you, live at peace with everyone. Do not take revenge my dear friends, but leave room for God's wrath, for it is written: "It is mine to avenge; I will repay," says the Lord. On the contrary:
"If your enemy is hungry, feed him,
if he is thirsty, give him something to drink.
In doing this, you will heap burning coals on his head."
Do not be overcome by evil, but overcome evil with good.

—Romans 12:14, 17-21

1. Where do your beliefs about forgiveness come from? Which, if any, misconceptions have you believed about forgiveness? How has believing these affected your willingness or ability to forgive?

2. Have you been harboring unforgiveness toward your abuser? If so, how has this affected you and those close to you?

3. Is it possible you may have committed sins as a result of the abuse you've suffered? If you are honest with yourself, what sins can you confess?

4. What tangible steps can you take to remember your abuser is also a human loved by God?

5. List some things you can thank God for even in the midst, and aftermath, of your abuse.

Journal Your Journey

6. *You might like to write a letter to your abuser or anyone else you have a hard time forgiving. You will not be sending the letter to this person, so feel free to write anything you want. Tell them how they*

have hurt you, how they made you feel, the losses you've incurred because of them. When the letter is finished, destroy it in a way that feels satisfying to you: rip it into a thousand pieces, burn it, bury it ... do whatever feels best. You may find this exercise liberates you from many of your negative feelings.

7. Do you struggle with forgiving yourself? If so, what do you believe you need to forgive yourself for?

8. If you have asked God's forgiveness, do you feel as if He's forgiven you?

9. In what ways can you or have you tried to make restitution for the wrongs you've committed?

10. Do you speak negatively to yourself? If so, do you think this is simply a bad habit, or are you fighting a spiritual battle? What spiritual weapons can you use to fight this battle? What friends can you ask to help you fight?

11. Which step(s) will you find hardest to take in your journey toward self-forgiveness? Which will you find the easiest?

CHAPTER 9

Bring God Glory as a Single Woman, and Use Wisdom in Dating

I delight greatly in the Lord;
my soul rejoices in my God.
For he has clothed me with garments of salvation
and arrayed me in a robe of his righteousness.

—Isaiah 61:10

Suddenly you are single again! You may have very mixed feelings about this. You may:

- be thrilled to be alone, now able to make your own choices without having to ask anyone's permission
- feel lonely and adrift, missing having a man in your life
- be surprised how much you miss your ex, the man who abused you
- not really care to be in a relationship, but miss having sex
- be fearful, wondering how you will provide for yourself and/or your children.

Maybe you feel something else, or all five of the above at different times! This is not unusual, and there is nothing wrong with you. You have been through a major trauma.

Take Time to Focus on Your Healing

Because of this, I encourage you to put new romantic relationships on hold for quite some time while you work on your healing process. Why?

First, investing yourself in a relationship with another man will take your time and attention away from doing the things you need to do for your healing. Healing from emotional abuse doesn't happen overnight. Healing is hard work and requires a great deal of emotional energy. Beginning a new love relationship also requires lots of emotional energy, but it is so much more fun, isn't it? Focusing your energy on a new man rather than on your painful feelings might seem to be the easier choice. However, if you don't spend your time focusing on your healing, this new relationship has little chance of survival, and you won't be any further along your journey to healing than before. If there is an amazing man who surfaces during this phase of your healing, you can trust that if loves you, he will wait for you to work on healing and even encourage you to do so.

If you have recently left your abuser, I encourage you not to begin a new romantic relationship right now for two reasons:

- You will not be able to fully focus on doing the work needed to heal from the abuse you've suffered.
- You may end up in another abusive relationship.

But even more important, if you haven't spent the time doing the healing you need, you may end up in another abusive relationship. Unlearning the life patterns that brought you to choose an abuser in the first place will take time. It is probable you learned these patterns as a child. Unlearning them will not be impossible, but it will take time, work, energy, and perseverance.

Being really alone may be a new sensation for you. I hadn't experienced it since I was a teenager. Because of my need to feel wanted, I had never gone more than two days without a boyfriend—there was always someone waiting in the wings. When I suddenly became single, my first reaction was complete joy! I had no overbearing, cruel person in my life telling me what to do. I could make any decision I wanted, go wherever I wanted, whenever I wanted. It was heaven!

However, in just a few months, a problem surfaced. I realized I missed the physical intimacy of marriage. I was growing my relationship with Jesus, but He wasn't there to hold me at night, and I was struggling. This was when I happened upon Joshua Harris's book *I Kissed Dating*

Goodbye.[81] It helped me point my eyes to the Lord during that difficult time. Harris encourages single people to take their eyes off the need to date and to enjoy their singleness—to use their time and energy for the Lord. He says when you begin to view singleness as a gift, you can learn to be content with having

> When you view singleness as a gift, you are able to focus on ministry and friendships with both men and women.

friendships instead of romantic relationships during the time God wants you to be single. This relieves your life of the waste of time and energy short-term relationships take. You are then able to focus on ministry and deepening friendships with men and women alike.

Perhaps you believe having sex outside of marriage is not a bad idea. You are no longer a virgin, and everyone does it, right? Harris writes about the beauty of purity and asks if you are willing to fight for it in your life. He writes, "Yes, it requires work. Purity doesn't happen by accident; it requires obedience to God, but this obedience is not burdensome or overbearing. We have only to consider the alternatives to impurity to see the beauty of walking in God's will. Impurity is a grimy film that coats the soul, a shadow that blocks light and darkens our countenance. God's love for the impure does not cease, but their ability to enjoy this love does. For in our impurity we are turned from Him. Sin and its defilement are never found near His throne; they can only gain advantage when we turn away from His radiance."[82]

Sex can be compared to a fire. Inside of marriage, sex is God's wonderful gift to two people, drawing them close together, sealing their union. This is like a fire kept inside a fireplace; it brings light and warmth to a home. Sex outside of marriage can be compared to lighting a fire in the middle of your living room. It soon gets out of control and has the potential to burn down the house and harm everyone in its path.

Harris writes, "Do you see the beauty and power and protection of purity? Do you want all this? Do you ache for it? Are you ready to deny yourself the pleasures of the moment to live a pure, God-focused life? May your love for Him fuel a lifelong, passionate pursuit of righteousness."[83]

But Doesn't the Lord Promise to Give You the Desires of Your Heart?

Yes, the Lord promises you the desires of your heart.

Delight yourself in the Lord and he will give you
the desires of your heart (Psalm 37:4, ESV).

Which leads to the question:

What *is* the desire of your heart?

My daughter dated a wonderful Christian boy throughout her first years in college. Our family fell in love with him. As she grew closer to the Lord, however, she realized his walk with God was not very strong, and she doubted he could be the spiritual leader of their home. As a result, they broke up for a year. During that period, Mark focused his time concentrating on his studies, growing his relationship with the Lord, and serving Him. He became exactly the type of spiritual leader my daughter hoped to marry. However, she had determined not to be anything more than friends with him until they both felt it was the Lord's will.

One day, Mark was in their church, a few seats down from my daughter. In agony he called out to the Lord, "Lord, why won't you give me the desire of my heart?" (Yes, he was thinking of my daughter.) He heard an audible voice say to him, "Mark, I AM the desire of your heart." Mark was moved to sobs in the middle of the church service. He realized the Lord really *was* the desire of his heart.

Shortly after this, both Mark and my daughter realized the Lord had answered their prayers. They had both matured and were ready to resume their relationship and move toward marriage. Their wedding day was one of the most joyous days of my life. To see two godly young people who had waited years for each other come together in purity moved many to tears.

So again I ask:

What is the desire of your heart?

Is the desire of your heart to have a beautiful, passionate, loving marriage to a man who will love you for the rest of your life? If so, I encourage you not to have sex again until you find a man who is worthy of your love, and who you can picture being happily married to for the rest of your life. Once you find him, I encourage you to wait to be sexu-

> If you desire a passionate, loving marriage for the rest of your life, I encourage you *not* to have sex again until you find a man worthy of your love, and you marry him.

ally intimate with him until you are actually married. Why?

Yes, this is God's plan, and yes, God knows best: after all, He created love, marriage, and sex. Even more than this, I can attest from personal experience the unbelievable passion two people can experience who really love each other yet wait until they marry to make love. None of the premarital sexual experiences I had before my first marriage, nor the sexual experiences I had with my first husband, can even compare with the fire my second husband and I experienced on our honeymoon and still experience today. Unmitigated joy. Yes, the months leading up to our wedding were difficult (*very* difficult), but the wait made the culmination so much better.

What if you are already in a sexual relationship? Is your future married life doomed to failure? *Not at all!* God is the God of grace. His love covers over a multitude of sins (1 Peter 4:8). Nevertheless, I would encourage you to strive for purity moving forward.

But How Do You Deal with Your Loneliness?

In her book *Single and Loving It! Living Life to the Fullest*, Kate McVeigh asks, "Have you ever started feeling so sorry for yourself that you played Elvis Presley's song, 'Are You Lonesome Tonight?' and spent the rest of the evening crying?"[84]

McVeigh writes that there is a difference between being alone and being lonely. She travels frequently and stays in hotels by herself and enjoys it. She enjoys her time alone with God, and you can too. James 4:8 says: *Come near to God and he will come near to you.*

As Christians, we have the Holy Spirit living inside of us; because of this, we are never truly alone. In Matthew 28:20 Jesus says, *"And surely I am with you always, to the very end of the age."*

The Holy Spirit wants to comfort you. As McVeigh writes: "Your life isn't over! God is a God of second, third, and fourth chances."[85]

Learning to be alone and content can be hard. It is a skill, and like any other skill, it takes practice. This will be a greater challenge for those who are extroverts. For you, finding women friends will be crucial.

The Lord Is Your Husband

You have likely heard that the church is "the bride of Christ." If we are His bride, then, for now, I recommend you consider Jesus your husband. When my second husband and I began seeing each other, I shared the book *I Kissed Dating Goodbye* with him. In return, he shared a poem[86] with me that he had been living by. We don't know who wrote it, but we have shared it with many single people who long for a spouse. It is about trusting God, allowing God to be your husband, and letting him give you full satisfaction. It remains meaningful to us today. God wants the best for you. Look to Him.

Spend Your Time as a Single Woman Making Yourself Valuable

McVeigh encourages single women to make themselves as valuable as they can to people around them. She describes a friend whose pastor husband died suddenly when he was only 37, leaving her with two young sons and a church to run. Instead of being overcome with fear and grief, or becoming bitter, she trusted God. She believed God would bring something positive out of a situation that seemed awful to her.

She developed the spiritual gifts God had given her while running the church for several years. Today, she travels and teaches how to raise children and overcome hard situations by trusting the Lord. At the same time, she developed her writing and administrative skills and became a blessing to many people. Being single didn't hold her back from becoming all she could be in God.[87]

Harris also encourages singles to be successful in this season of their lives. He writes:

> Until you realize God's gift of your singleness, you'll probably miss out on the incredible opportunities it holds. Perhaps even now you can think of an opportunity you could grasp if you let go of the dating mind-set. As a single you have the freedom right now to explore, study, and tackle the world.[88]

My Joy in Being Single

I will give you an example of one of the ways the Lord blessed me and allowed me to be a blessing to others during my time as a single woman of God. I love to travel, but traveling was very painful with my ex-husband, so I didn't travel often. Friends from church had twice gone to a third world country on a weeklong mission trip, but I never felt I should go. After I became single, I suddenly had every other week alone since my children were staying with their father half the time. When my church began planning another mission trip, I signed up to go.

This was my first such trip. Because I did not receive an audible word from the Lord telling me I should go, I spent several weeks wondering if I should back out. I asked myself many times: *What do I have to offer?* Finally, I remembered Jesus asking all Christians to *"Go and make disciples of all nations"* (Matthew 28:20). Even though I did not feel specifically called to go, I was not disobeying the Lord in joining my friends. I packed my duffel bag and climbed on the bus.

> As a single, you have the freedom to explore, study, and tackle the world.

One day on the trip, we visited an orphanage. I immediately fell in love with the children. I felt as if my heart was ripping from my body when it was time to leave. I decided I wanted to return soon. I went home and began learning to speak the language of the children. I learned I had a gift for languages!

I found I had other hidden gifts. In the previous few years I had taken up painting as a hobby and begun to learn to play the piano. Even though my skills were limited in these areas, the Lord was able to use my willingness to bless the children in these areas as well. This one short mission trip turned into a long-term ministry that lasted many years. The Lord opened His world for me to see and love these people. It has blessed me beyond measure. What a great God we serve!

Perhaps Your Sole Mission Right Now Is Raising Your Children

Perhaps you read the above sections and wonder how you will ever have time to go to the bathroom alone, much less travel on mission trips or become a public speaker! If you are raising small children by yourself,

> Raising godly children is the highest calling God has ever given.

this goal probably seems unattainable. Most days you drag your body out of bed, dress everyone, get them to school and yourself to work, come home, cook a quick dinner, throw a load of laundry in the washer, help with homework, and drop into bed exhausted.

Remember, though, that raising godly children is the highest calling the Lord has ever asked of someone. If this is the season of life you find yourself in, rest assured God is mightily pleased with all your efforts. Seasons are only seasons, and they are temporary. King Solomon said in Ecclesiastes Chapter 3:

There is a time for everything,
and a season for every activity under heaven:
a time to be born and a time to die,
a time to plant and a time to uproot . . .
a time to scatter stones and a time to gather them,
a time to embrace and a time to refrain.

Though you may feel overwhelmed with your role as a single parent, God will bless you for your obedience to Him in this most important work.

A Prayer for the Single Woman

In *Single and Loving It,* McVeigh writes several prayers for the single woman. The following prayer from McVeigh greatly touched me:

Father, thank You that this is the day You have made. I will rejoice and be glad in it! My joy is in You, and You are working Your plan in perfect timing. I will take advantage of this season of being single and devote more time to You. I'll delight myself in seeking You, and I know You will reward me and give me the desires of my heart. I'll dedicate myself to being a blessing to others, and I know that when I help to make things happen for others, you can make things happen for me.[89]

Seeking God's Wisdom in Dating

Daughters of Jerusalem, I charge you
by the gazelles and by the does of the field:
Do not arouse or awaken love
until it so desires (Song of Solomon 2:7).

If you're divorced as a result of domestic abuse, can you remarry? It's a difficult question, to be certain. I recommend you seek God and draw your own conclusions. For me, based on my study of the Bible, and with the help of the study of several theologians, I believe domestic abuse is a valid biblical reason for a Christian abuse victim to divorce. Once an abuse victim is divorced, I believe she has a biblical right to remarry. I wrote two chapters (Chapters 22 and 33) to discuss what the Bible says about divorce and remarriage in my first book, *A Journey through*

> I believe domestic abuse is a valid biblical reason for a Christian abuse victim to divorce. Once divorced, I believe she has a biblical right to remarry.

Emotional Abuse: from Bondage to Freedom. You may wish to review those chapters.

Each woman needs to search her own heart and decide for herself whether she believes God gives her the go-ahead to remarry in such a situation. Psalm 139:23, 24 says:

Search me, God, and know my heart;
test me and know my anxious thoughts.
See if there is any offensive way in me,
and lead me in the way everlasting.

If you don't have peace with the Lord about remarrying, it would not be right for you *in your own eyes* to pursue a romantic relationship with another man. Until and unless God changes your heart and gives you peace about remarrying, I recommend you spend your time as a single woman bringing glory to God. But what if . . .

What If You Have Peace in Your Heart About Beginning Another Relationship?

If your divorce is actually final, and if you feel it would not be a sin for you to remarry, or you would be marrying for the first time, you still need to decide if dating is wise for you at this time. How would you discern this? I can't answer for you, but here are two categories of questions to think through.

1. Have you progressed far enough in your healing to consider another relationship?

- Do you spend a lot of time each day thinking about your ex?

- Are you still very angry with him, or do you often think about getting revenge for the pain he's caused you?

- Are you suffering from serious anxiety or depression? (Some amount of this is to be expected.)

- Are your children unstable and needing a great deal of your time and attention?

- Are you looking for someone to: build your self-esteem, protect you from your ex, or help you financially?

- Do you want someone to help you forget the pain of the past, or do you believe that once you marry you won't have to continue doing the hard work of healing from your abuse?

If you answered yes to any of these questions, I encourage you not to begin dating yet, and to continue working on your healing. You and/or your children are probably not ready.

2. Are you ready to commit to a relationship?

I answer this question differently than many people do. Like Harris, author of *I Kissed Dating Goodbye*, I don't believe in "dating" in the way most people in the modern western world understand the term. Today, most people jump quickly into romance because it feels good. Often, this includes sexual intercourse, and sometimes on the first date. There is little consideration about whether this person is the one God has chosen for a lifetime. People rarely think about what is best for the *other* person.

Instead, romance is too often enjoyed for romance's sake, no matter what the cost is for those involved. Couples often move in together with no discussion of marriage. Two, three, even five years later, they are still living together. In the United States, by the year 2010, 40 percent of all children were born outside of marriage.[90] This is not the way God designed romance and the family to work.

> Three major questions to consider before you begin dating:
>
> 1. Do you feel a peace from the Lord about (re)marrying?
> 2. Have you progressed far enough in your healing?
> 3. Are you ready to commit to a relationship?

I believe a person has no business dating someone unless they are willing and able to marry him or her within a fairly short amount of time, within approximately one year. I realize to some, this is a radical position, but let me explain.

To begin a relationship with someone you don't ever intend to marry is simply playing with someone else's heart for your enjoyment. Often when you do this you will also unexpectedly be hurt in the process because you will become emotionally involved whether you expect to or not.

To begin a relationship with someone who doesn't ever intend to marry you is perhaps even worse. Often a man won't advertise the fact he isn't serious about marriage. Here are some tips, however, to help you identify these types of men.

In his book *Boy Meets Girl: Say Hello to Courtship*,[91] Joshua Harris introduces the "old-fashioned" concept of courtship. Though courtship brings to mind horse and buggy days, I believe courtship can be extremely helpful for today's Christians, especially for women who have been abused. Simply put, in courtship,

The joy of intimacy is the reward of commitment.

It is a relationship between a man and a woman who are actively and intentionally together to consider marrying each other. It combines biblical principles of loving each other as you love yourself, the priority of sexual purity, and the need for the wisdom and perspective that comes from having a relationship within a loving community of other Christians.

> The words you use to describe your dating process don't matter as much as how you live. Are you trying to honor God, or are you just out for a good time?

Harris describes asking his future wife out on their first date, and then asking whether he could court her. My relationship with my second husband didn't happen that way. We had known each other for more than a year as friends in an adult Sunday school class. We went out on a few dates and decided we could potentially have a future together. We then dated seriously, and exclusively, for about four months before we officially began courting each other. Harris writes—and I agree—that the words you use to describe your dating process don't matter as much as the way you live. Are you trying to honor God with your dating life, or are you just looking for romance?

In summary, dating should have a purpose; that is, one should date in preparation for marriage. The hearts of most women want the fairy tale, the happily-ever-after love that lasts a lifetime. Many of us have given up on this hope because of the abuse we've experienced. Keep reading; I believe your hope can be reborn.

If you *are* ready to date . . .

How Can You Meet the Right Man?

My husband and I have a godly female friend we both admire, Elizabeth.

She is the most intelligent, gifted woman I've ever met. Elizabeth had planned to be a medical doctor until she became a Christian. She dated for years; she had many friends trying to set her up with their single friends.

After becoming a Christian, she changed her plans and decided to go to seminary to become a pastor. Since she was entering a school full of single Christian men, she committed to God that she would look at every man as her brother until He changed her heart. It freed her from the weight of looking at these single men as potential husbands.

Once she graduated from seminary, she worked as a youth pastor for several years. She never dated, never searched for a husband, and never worried whether she would end up alone. Many years passed. She visited an African country on a short-term mission trip, and there she met a godly, caring African native man. She never expected to see him again. But God had other plans.

Two years later, when Elizabeth approached her thirtieth birthday, God called her to move to Africa as a full-time missionary. I remember saying at the time, "I guess Elizabeth will remain single for the rest of her life." My husband had more faith. He said, "If the Lord means for her to marry, he can bring her a Christian husband even in Africa." My husband was right. She was reunited with the man she'd met on her first trip. They remained friends for two years—until God opened their eyes to each other as potential mates. Though they had many hurdles to overcome and came from two very different cultures, as well as both being raised in broken homes, today they are happily married and working side by side for the Lord.

> You are worthy of being loved by an honorable, caring Christian man. If God plans for you to marry, he will bring you a husband worthy of you.

I realize every woman who is reading this book is not an Elizabeth. I know I certainly did not have her level of faith and patience when I was single. However, I want to encourage every Christian woman reading this book. God loves you and wants the best for you. He considered you worthy of sending His Son to die for you. You are therefore worthy of being loved by an honorable, caring Christian man. I believe if God plans for you to marry, He will bring you a husband who is worthy of you.

And I also believe there are many men (of the approximate three and a half billion men on earth) who could be a good husband for you. Even our friend Elizabeth did not sit at home waiting for her husband to knock on her door. Though she wasn't searching for a husband, she lived a full, productive life where she met and worked with many available single men. I think you will increase your odds, and your general life happiness, if you put yourself in situations where you can meet many different people.

I highly recommend you do *not* try to meet your future husband in a bar; this should be obvious. Spend your time in the places you would like your future husband to hang out. If you want him to be a churchgoer, find a Bible-believing church, join a Sunday school class for singles, and get involved. Do this not just to find a husband, but also to make friends with other Christians. If you have children and you'd like to marry a man with kids, join the PTA or go to the park or the pool or even Chuck E. Cheese with your kids! You will see how potential dates treat their children. If you are a cyclist, join a cycling group. Are you a hiker, painter, or writer? Most recreation centers have groups or inexpensive classes in all these areas. If you currently do none of these things but want to learn, join a class! Even if you don't meet a husband, your life will be enriched.

The great thing about meeting a potential husband in a group is you will get a chance to become friends with him first, to see how he treats his friends. Is he kind and thoughtful, or is he a jerk? Is he responsible, someone others count on? Does he show up on time? My husband tells our teens you can discern almost everything you need to know about a potential mate as a friend before you have a single date with him. The only thing you can't know for sure is whether he will be abusive. Usually, you can't tell if someone will be abusive toward you until you begin dating him, because an abuser won't act in a controlling manner toward you until you move toward an exclusive relationship. However, there are some red flags you can look for even when you are still just friends:

> You can discern *almost* everything you need to know about a man as a friend before you date him.

- Does he blame others for his mistakes?

- Does he always have to be right?

- Does he refuse to apologize and admit he is wrong?

- Does he talk about himself all the time, or does he listen to others, even those he can't date?

- Does he get insulted easily? Does he get angry about things that most people take in stride?

- Does he tease animals or children or expect more of them than they are capable?

- Does he believe in rigid sex roles; i.e., women should "always" stay at home, do all the cooking, cleaning, child care, etc?

> There are many red flags you can watch for before you date someone to discern if they have the potential to be abusive.

- Has he been involved in any abusive relationships in the past, even if it was "her fault," or he claims he was the victim?

- Does he ever use force in an argument, even with friends?

- Does he have a poor relationship with his family?

What About Online Dating?

I know many people have found their mates through online dating sites, but I am not a fan. For one thing, with online dating, you will have a difficult time getting to know him as a friend, or watching him with others, before you actually date. Second, I know several women have said the men they came in contact with made them feel "dirty." One or two said they later found out some of the men they dated were already married! Last, it is difficult to remain safe when you begin dating someone you know nothing about—except what he says about himself on a computer screen.

However, I do know a few couples that met via online sites and are happily married, and I know that with God nothing is impossible (Luke 1:37). I would encourage you to try to meet men in a more traditional way and wait on the Lord before signing up for an online dating service. If you do eventually join one, look for a Christian site that is above board and has many safety guidelines. If you decide to date online, I recommend you only date someone who lives near you. If you begin a long-distance relationship, you may invest too much of your time and emotional energy before you are able to meet him, and you will have very little chance to know his family and friends.

Safety Guidelines

I recommend you do a background check on anyone you consider dating. This will help you discern whether this person is married, has a criminal record, or has gone bankrupt in the past.

If you decide to date someone you don't know well, whether you meet online or in the grocery store, I recommend you take precautions to keep yourself safe. Begin dating casually, and in the daytime. Pick a public place to meet; perhaps ask him to join you and a group of friends in an activity. The right man will be happy to do this. Drive yourself there, and drive yourself home. Never invite him to your home, or go to his—until you know him well. Too many women have been raped on dates this way. For your next four or five dates, continue meeting him in public places and do group activities with your friends and his. This will allow you to observe how he interacts with others and what type of friends he has. Your friends will be able to tell you what they think of him. Often those closest to us can discern things about potential mates we cannot see. If your friends don't like him, listen to them. There are plenty of men out there! I firmly believe you can be happier alone than together with the wrong man; and if you've been emotionally abused, you certainly have experienced being with the wrong man. You may feel awkward dating this way at first, but I believe you will see the fruit of this approach in the long run.

> Be extremely cautious if you date someone you don't know well. *Never* go home with him on the first date.

What if your friends love him and you don't? Listen to your instincts! The point of having friends and family along is to help you weed out the riffraff, not to talk you into dating someone who creeps you out.

Make a Potential Husband 'Run the Gauntlet'

In her book, *Dating After Trauma: How to Find the Love of Your Life After Experiencing an Abusive Relationship, Rape, or Sexual Abuse*, Emily Avagliano describes the way she dated after suffering sexual trauma. She required her dates to "run the gauntlet." What does this mean? In Roman and English armies, it was a way for a condemned soldier to redeem himself—by running through two rows of his fellow soldiers who would beat him. If he made it to the end, he could rejoin his comrades with a clean slate.[92] Avagliano uses the term in a much less repellant way. She writes that she required her husband to pass a test before she would agree to marry him. He had to pass through the gauntlet to win her heart. She required her dates to pass through a series of steps before they could reach intimacy or engage in heavy conversation with her.[93] This is similar counsel to Harris's advice in *Boy Meets Girl.* Both books look at dating from the perspective that the man must win the woman's heart; she is not responsible for "catching" him.

Remind yourself God loves you, wants the best for you, and you are worthy of marrying a kind, respectful, loving man. Focus on whether he is good enough for *you*, not whether you are good enough for *him*. When you are with him, don't ask yourself whether he likes you; ask yourself whether you like him. This is another reason it is important to heal from your past abuse before dating. You need to have healthy self-esteem so you can believe you are worthy of being pursued in a godly manner. Avagliano writes:

> Healthy men love women who respect themselves.

> Healthy men love women who respect themselves. If you focus on him, his reactions to you, preventing a breakup, and the possibility of getting hurt, you will appear needy and controlling, and the relationship will slip through your fingers.[94]

Be willing to tell him no if you don't like something, even if it is a restaurant he suggests. If he does something you don't like, tell him right away. If he gets upset, he is not your husband. You don't need to be with someone who can't hear no; you have already tried that!

Abusive men will attempt to rush you into a relationship. Healthy men will take their time. They will remain engaged and interested but won't pressure you to commit to them in the first few dates. This is because, unlike abusive men who are looking for someone to control, healthy men are looking for someone to love.

When you begin seeing him, you may not fall in love right away. This is OK. Don't get upset if you don't immediately feel strong emotions toward him. Your feelings may grow over time. Just ask yourself if he could be a good friend.

Avagliano's next advice sounds old-fashioned, but is for our protection, and actually works: let *him* be the leader. Don't be the instigator in the relationship; let him suggest what you do. Don't feel you need to help him; he's a big boy! If he can't lead you when you begin dating, he won't be able to be the spiritual leader of your home either. If you help him through the gauntlet, you are reacting out of fear that no good man will ever want to marry you, and you are willing to settle for less than your standards. This lowers your self-esteem and makes you look desperate and less attractive to him at the same time.

Let him do something nice for you, and you can then do something nice in return. For example, he calls you; you call him back. He tells you about his childhood, you tell him something about yours. Don't vomit every bad thing that ever happened; reveal a bit about yourself. He brings you flowers, you bake him cookies. And so on.

Dating after being abused is scary. You may wonder how you'll know if you are picking an abuser again. If he is willing to run the gauntlet, there is less chance you are dating an abuser. Avagliano says she dated many men who failed the gauntlet before she met and married her husband.

> Letting him be the instigator in the dating process allows you to decide whether he is good enough for *you.*

Women who are happily married will tell you two things about their husbands:

• Dating them was easy.

• "He was so nice to me, I knew he was different."[95]

I can affirm this. My second husband is as different from my first husband as day is to night. When I dated my first husband, everything was difficult. He argued about everything. I felt I had to constantly explain my motives and actions. My second husband trusted me from the first day. He had reasonable boundaries with me and allowed me to have reasonable boundaries with him. He didn't pick fights for no reason; we rarely argued. He was kind and polite and thoughtful. Dating him was a joy. Being married to him is also a joy. God is so good!

Avagliano contrasts unhealthy men to healthy men.[96] She says an unhealthy man will rush you to be emotionally or sexually intimate. He won't call when he says he will. He will often call you and want to see you *right then*, and then won't call for days or weeks. He will claim to have certain values but will act completely differently with you, or brag about treating someone else badly in the past (but claim it will never happen with you). He is emotionally immature. He doesn't want to talk about your relationship; he will always want to keep you guessing. If you share your feelings, he will withdraw from you. He has few friends, or you dislike his friends. He dislikes your friends and family and tries to keep you from them. He treats those he considers "lower" than himself (like waiters or janitors) poorly. He is jealous of other men you come in contact with for no reason. He wants to know where you are at all times. When he gets angry, he blames his anger on you. Look again at this list; it describes men who are apt to become abusers. Keep away from men like this!

In contrast, a healthy man earns the right to be your best friend by his constant, good behavior. He does not rush you either emotionally or sexually. He takes the relationship slowly, but is always interested. He calls you and asks you out again very soon after your last date. He is trustworthy. The way he describes himself equates to the way he acts toward you. You feel safe around him. He is thoughtful of your wants and needs. He wants to know more about you, what you think, how you feel. If you set a boundary with him, he doesn't withdraw, but immediately corrects his behavior or works for a healthy compromise. He apologizes if he makes a mistake. He has many deep relationships with friends and family that you like. He likes your friends and family and allows you to spend time with them, even if it takes time away from him. He doesn't blame you for his bad behavior.

> A healthy man is thoughtful, trustworthy, doesn't rush you or blame you for his bad behavior, apologizes if he makes a mistake, and likes your friends and family.

Keep in mind you are looking for a real human being. Your future husband will not be perfect, just as you are not perfect. He will have flaws. Just make sure he is healthy and willing to own his mistakes and make changes for you.

How Should You Include Your Kids?

I recommend you wait to introduce your children to your potential mate until you are fairly certain you will marry. This is to protect your blooming relationship, but mainly to protect your children. Your kids have been through a lot of emotional upheaval in their lives already. They no longer have their original "intact" family unit, so they have suffered the loss of living with both parents. Even if the other parent was abusive, this is a great loss. In addition, they have lived with domestic abuse. Whether their father abused them or not, the abuse you experienced will have affected them in many ways.

They have their own healing to do. They may have trouble attaching to new adults in their lives. Bringing a potential mate into their life that eventually leaves will be another loss for them. The more people they bond to and later lose, the more trauma they experience. The more men you date and introduce your kids to, the harder time your kids may have bonding with them as they get their hopes dashed again and again.

> Wait to meet each other's kids until you are fairly certain you will marry each other. This protects your kids and your relationship.

On the other side, your children may hate the idea of you dating and remarrying anyone. Women often use their children as a kind of barometer, helping them decide whether to marry someone. If your children have decided they don't want you to remarry, they may do everything in their power to sabotage your budding relationship. You may mistakenly think there is something wrong with your fellow, and let a wonderful man go, when in reality the children would treat anyone poorly at first.

My advice is to carry on your dating life apart from your children as much as you possibly can. Meet him at a neutral place as long as you need to, protecting your relationship and your kids. When you have decided he is the one—and he has shown he is serious about you—then you can introduce him to the children. Both of you should be prepared for the chance your children will react badly. If they do, you will need to work through this together. Don't wait so long to introduce them that the wedding plans are already made and cannot be changed. You don't know how long you all may need to get used to each other.

When Your Potential Mate Meets Your Kids—Or You Meet His

Everyone is likely to be nervous. Allow the first meeting to be short and in a comfortable place. If you have small children, don't take them to a fancy restaurant and expect them to be on best behavior for two hours the first time they meet. That is begging for disaster. Ask your date to be respectful and interested but not to immediately act like your kids' best friend. He isn't their father, and they may never treat him that way. Right now, he is simply a friend of yours who wants to get to know them as people.

I find adults often don't know how to treat children with respect as people. Sometimes adults are overly friendly with kids, calling them "pal" or "buddy" the first time they meet. Kids hate this. Often adults will try to buy a child's affection by bringing them gifts or taking them out for ice cream or junk food every time they are together. Children may like the gifts, but will often have no respect for a person like this.

Alternatively, potential stepparents may try to assume a parental role way too early in the relationship, ordering the child around before the couple is even married, mistakenly believing they must "lay down the law" right away. This is also a big mistake. If the child is in your date's home, he can set appropriate boundaries about rules in his home, such as "no jumping on the couch," or "don't pull the dog's tail," but ask him not to go overboard. Ask him to say please and thank you to your kids, just as you will ask your kids to do the same.

> When meeting each other's kids, don't be overly friendly, buy their affection, or treat them the way a parent would treat them.

When my second husband and I were dating, I used to bring a board game or two with me to his house when I knew his kids would be there. We would sometimes have a meal together, and then we would play a game or two. If his older kids didn't want to play, we didn't force them. Playing the game gave us a chance to talk while doing something else, taking away some of the awkwardness. (When it was time for me to leave, I took the games back home.)

Adjustments You Will All Need to Make

After a few months, I realized that when I asked my kids to do something, I never said please and thank you. We didn't consider this rude; it was just how we did things in our family. His kids thought this was terribly rude of me. They mentioned this to my soon-to-be-husband, who gently mentioned it to me when we were alone. I was a bit hurt, and felt somewhat defensive. Why should I, as the adult, have to say please?

Then I realized: why shouldn't I? I quickly added please and thank you around his kids, and around mine as well! This is just one small example of the ways our families had to adjust to each other when we got married and combined our households. If you and your potential husband are unwilling or unable to make these types of adjustments for each other and each other's kids, your marriage will not be peaceful.

Summary

Being alone after an abusive relationship can be difficult, yet spending enough time alone before entering into another relationship is important for your healing. While you are waiting, you can enjoy this time if you focus on honoring God and living for Him.

Dating again after being abused can be confusing. There are many things to consider:

- Do you feel peace with the Lord about (re)marrying?

- Have you progressed far enough in your healing to consider another relationship?

- Are you ready to commit to a relationship?

- What steps will you take to find a good man?

- How do you know if he will be abusive or not?

- Should you let him do all the leading?

- When do you introduce him to your kids?

I pray after reading this chapter you will be more at peace with the dating process. If you feel ready to date, I hope you know how much God loves you and wants the best for you. If it is His will for you to (re)marry, please know you are worthy of finding a wonderful, kind man who will love and honor you.

A Drink of Water for the Journey

We all long for love, and sometimes
we struggle with loneliness.

The Lord replies:

"And I will betroth you to me forever.

*I will betroth you to me in righteousness and in justice, in
steadfast love and in mercy."*

—HOSEA 2:19, ESV

1. Do you see wisdom in waiting to begin a new romantic relationship until you have spent time working on your healing? Why or why not?

2. Do you believe waiting to have sex until marriage is right for you? Explain.

3. Do you struggle with loneliness? How have you dealt with this?

4. What opportunities might you have if you remain single? Are there things you've wanted to try but have never had the opportunity? Travel, hobbies, schooling, ministry, others?

5. Do you believe you have progressed enough in your healing to consider dating?

6. Do you agree with the author that a Christian should only date if they plan to marry within a reasonable amount of time? Why or why not?

7. Do you worry about choosing another abusive partner? What can you do to prevent this?

8. Do you like the idea of having a potential mate "run the gauntlet"? What do you think this should look like?

9. Do you see wisdom in waiting to meet each other's children until you are fairly certain you will marry each other? Why or why not?

CHAPTER 10

Take Cautious Steps Toward Marriage

*... as a bridegroom adorns his head like a priest,
and as a bride adorns herself with her jewels.*

—Isaiah 61:10

Marrying—whether again, or for the first time—after being abused is a huge step. By marrying, you can set yourself up to become a victim again, or you can receive great healing. Which will it be? Much depends on how you go about the dating process, who you choose to marry, and how healed you are *before* you marry. But please realize this: if you expect your new husband to heal all your wounds from your past relationship(s), your marriage is doomed to fail.

This doesn't mean you must be completely healed in order to marry. I believe none of us are ever completely healed this side of Heaven. I certainly wasn't when I married my second husband. We live in a world full of broken people. Even your husband will be broken, whether or not he has experienced abuse. The fact we are all broken is the reason Jesus came to earth to die.

> When you marry after being abused, you may become a victim again, or receive great healing. Don't expect your new husband to heal all the wounds from your previous abusive relationship.

While Jesus was having dinner at Matthew's

house, many tax collectors and sinners came and ate with him and his disciples. When the Pharisees saw this, they asked his disciples, "Why does your teacher eat with tax collectors and sinners?"

On hearing this, Jesus said, "It is not the healthy who need a doctor, but the sick. But go and learn what this means: 'I desire mercy, not sacrifice.' For I have not come to call the righteous, but sinners" (Matthew 9:10-13).

And in Luke 19:10 Jesus said: *"For the Son of Man came to seek and to save the lost."*

Poor Reasons for Marrying

If you are looking to your new husband to make you feel good about yourself after your abuse, please don't get married. If you are looking to him as your sole sense of protection and comfort, please don't get married. If you are looking at him as a meal ticket, as someone to provide a roof over your head, please don't get married. Why not? You might believe you *need* someone to make you feel good about yourself after all you've been through. You might legitimately need protection and comfort, and you might need help with finances. These are not good reasons to marry, however. Marriages built on foundations such as these will not last. They will cause you, he, and any children you may have more pain than you have already experienced.

> Marrying because you are looking for a husband to make you feel good about yourself, to help you with finances, or to provide you with protection and comfort—none of these are good reasons to get married.

Good Reasons for Marrying

Why should you marry? And whom should you marry? Our culture would answer: "You should marry for love." But how do we define love? Is love that butterfly-in-your-stomach feeling you get when he walks into a room? Is it sexual tension whenever he is around? Is it the feeling of not being able to think about anyone or anything else day or night? What I've just described is infatuation, not love.

So, what is love? I'm going to describe something that sounds really unromantic, but it's critical to understand. Love is an action. Many couples have 1 Corinthians 13 read at their wedding ceremony. Why? I believe they understand this Bible passage describes true love . . . love as an action. On the face of it, 1 Corinthians 13:4-7 may not sound very romantic, but think about living day to day with a man who behaves toward you in this way:

> *Love is patient, love is kind.*
> *It does not envy, it does not boast, it is not proud.*
> *It does not dishonor others, it is not self-seeking,*
> *it is not easily angered, it keeps no record of wrongs.*
> *Love does not delight in evil but rejoices with the truth.*
> *It always protects, always trusts, always hopes, always perseveres.*

Sounds pretty romantic to me. I should know; I am married to a man like this. One of my husband's favorite sayings is "love is not a feeling; it's an action." Perhaps you are thinking: I don't deserve to marry a man like that! If you believe this, I recommend you remain single! If you believe you don't deserve a man like this, you will most likely not marry one, and any man who treats you less than this is not worth marrying. Also, if you believe you don't deserve a man like this, you probably have more healing to do before you marry. I recommend you continue on your journey to healing before you ask another person to share his life with you—for your sake and for his!

> If you believe you don't deserve to marry a man who will treat you well, I recommend you remain single. You may have more healing to do.

If you expect to marry a man who will treat you as 1 Corinthians 13 describes, you should expect to treat him the same way. This means that on a day-to-day basis you will be patient and kind toward him. You will put away your pride if you get into a disagreement and be the one to apologize first. You will not keep a running record of all his faults, and you won't blow up at the slightest provocation. You will hold onto hope when things look dismal—and persevere when you feel like leaving.

So the first reason to marry is if you can love him with action, and he can love you the same way.

The second reason to marry is if you and your future spouse will bring each other closer to the Lord. If you are a Christian woman, you should

> Two good reasons to marry: If you can love each other with action, and if you will bring each other closer to the Lord.

never marry a non-Christian man. The Bible is absolutely clear on this point.

Do not be yoked together with unbelievers. For what do righteousness and wickedness have in common? Or what fellowship can light have with darkness? What harmony is there between Christ and Belial? Or what does a believer have in common with an unbeliever? What agreement is there between the temple of God and idols? For we are the temple of the living God. As God has said:

*"I will live with them
and walk among them,
and I will be their God,
and they will be my people."
Therefore,
"Come out from them
and be separate,"
says the Lord.
"Touch no unclean thing,
and I will receive you."
And,
"I will be a Father to you,
and you will be my sons and daughters,"
says the Lord Almighty (2 Corinthians 6:14-18).*

The apostle Paul wrote these important words. Many will say you can marry a non-Christian and still have a happy marriage. If you are a true follower of Jesus, however, this will cause your marriage problems. There is a reason Paul made this exhortation as strongly as he did. No greater bond exists on earth than that of a man and woman in marriage. The marriage covenant is created so that *the two will become one flesh* (Genesis 2:24). As Christians, our primary love relationship should be with God. Another growing Christian will understand and encourage this, but a non-Christian never will. He will tolerate it, ignore it, or be envious of it. Your love of God will become a sore subject between you and your husband for the rest of your life. Rather than bonding the two of you closer, it will pull you apart. You will have to choose between drawing closer to your Lord or closer to your husband, a choice no wife should have to make. Jesus said:

> *"No one can serve two masters. Either you will hate the one and love the other, or you will be devoted to the one and despise the other" (Matthew 6:24).*

I have known many Christian women who have married seemingly decent and good non-Christian men. It has rarely turned out happily. Yes, some of them managed to keep their marriages together—but there was always a cost. Either the wife stepped back from her devotion to the Lord or her husband ridiculed her for her faith. In other cases, the marriage came apart. Marriage is difficult enough; don't begin one with such an important difference between you.

Sometimes a man will pretend he is a Christian while you are dating but not have a real commitment to the Lord. As soon as the marriage vows are said, he stops going to church, reading the Bible, and praying. He gives lip service to faith but lives like a nonbeliever. How can you discern whether the man you plan to marry is one of these men? Here are some questions to ask him, his family, friends, and yourself.

- Did he go to a church regularly *before* you began dating?

- Did he mostly surround himself with Christian friends or non-Christian friends?

- Did he take part in any group Bible study, accountability group, or life group?

- What were his favorite free time activities? Going to bars? Watching sports? Church or volunteer activities?

- Where did he go on vacation? Did he go to Las Vegas and gamble? Or on mission trips?

How he behaved *before* he knew you is a good indication of how he will behave *after* you get married.

Even if he is a Christian, you still need to consider this question: does your relationship bring each other closer to the Lord? Perhaps

> How your potential husband behaved *before* you met is a good indication of how he will behave *after* you are married.

191

you are so consumed with your physical attraction to him you cannot focus on spiritual things when you are together. Perhaps you bring out the worst in each other—your immaturity, jealousy, and quarrelsomeness. After you have spent some time together, compare your relationship with the Lord now to your relationship with the Lord before you met. Do you desire the Lord more now than before? Do you know Him better, love Him more? How about your intended husband? Has his relationship with the Lord grown stronger? If the answer to these questions is no, your relationship with God and each other will not grow stronger after you are married.

Once You Take the Plunge

Once you marry, you and your new husband have made a covenant with God. This is a very serious matter! I've heard people say shortly after they marry: "It just wasn't God's will for us to be together." Well, it *is* God's will after you marry. Jesus said: *"No one who puts a hand to the plow and looks back is fit for service in the kingdom of God"* (Luke 9:62).

Don't look back, look forward. Give your marriage your all. Forsake all others—except the Lord, of course—putting God first and your husband second.

What If He Is Abusive?

If you find your new husband is becoming abusive, do something about it *right away*. Don't sit around hoping you are mistaken, or hoping the problem will go away. The longer you wait, the larger the problem will grow. If your life or the lives of your children are in danger, call the National Domestic Violence Hotline at 1–800–799–SAFE(7233) or TTY 1–800–787–3224.[97] Ask them to help you make a safety plan and leave as soon as you safely can. If you are not in imminent danger, I recommend you read my first book, *A Journey through Emotional Abuse: from Bondage to Freedom*. I walk you through the steps you can take to stand up to the abuse, and then determine whether the marriage is worth fighting for.

> If you find your new husband is becoming abusive, do something about it *right away.*

Love and Respect

A popular, wonderful Christian marriage book is *Love and Respect:*

The Love She Most Desires, The Respect He Desperately Needs by Dr. Emerson Eggerichs.[98] The premise of the book is that women need to feel loved and men need to feel respected. Of course, women also need to feel respected and men need to feel loved, but this is not their first need. Eggerichs opines that if a man does not feel respected, he will have a difficult time showing love to his wife, and a woman who does not feel loved will have difficulty showing respect to her husband.

I can attest to this. Early in my second marriage, my family came over for dinner. I asked my husband how long and at what temperature I should bake the potatoes. He told me what he thought, but I disagreed. I made the mistake of mentioning this in front of my entire family. Later, I couldn't find my husband; he had gone missing for more than an hour. I had embarrassed him in front of everyone. He felt disrespected and deeply hurt.

Later, he asked me why I bothered asking him how long to bake the potatoes if I already knew the answer. I apologized with tears. I realized this was a habit I had started with my first husband. I always asked him how to do the most minor tasks in order to prevent him from getting mad at me. However, in my second marriage, I wanted to do things my way. So, even though I asked my second husband his thoughts, I always did what I thought was right. I merely wanted him to confirm my opinions because I was unsure of myself.

> If a man does not feel respected, he won't show love to his wife. If she doesn't feel loved, she won't show him respect.

I learned a valuable lesson that day. I now do my very best to never embarrass him in public. But more than that, I try very hard to show him respect in everything I do.

In the same way, my husband has learned how hurt I get if he answers a question I ask with even the slightest edge to his voice. To me, the edge in his voice reminds me of the verbal abuse I experienced in my first marriage, and this seems unloving.

Ephesians 5: Submission, Really?

The apostle Paul talks about love and respect in Ephesians 5:21-33. It's possible you despise these verses because they were used to spiritually abuse you in your former relationship. My first husband also used these verses to hurt me, and keep me in bondage. However, I believe these thirteen verses best describe God's perfect plan for marriage. Are you willing to look at them again with new eyes to see what the Bible says about the husband/wife relationship?

The first thing to note is that submission is not the same thing as obedience. Obedience comes from the word obey, which is defined by *Merriam-Webster's 11th Collegiate Dictionary* as:

> *Obey*: to follow the commands or guidance of; to conform to or comply with (as in "obey an order")

Submission comes from the word submit, which is defined by the same dictionary as:

> *Submit*: to yield oneself to the authority or will of another; to defer to or consent; to abide by the opinion or authority of another

A person *obeys* because they have no choice; they are being commanded, or ordered to conform, as a child obeys a parent or a marine obeys his sergeant. However, *submission* implies that a person chooses to yield themselves to the will of another; they consent of their own free will. A Christian woman therefore would choose to defer her will to that of her husband out of love for him and love for and trust in the Lord Jesus Christ.

> A woman submits when she chooses to yield herself to the will of another person out of her own free will.

Ephesians 5 is often used to describe submission for women only. However, it really describes submission for all. Paul's discussion on marriage begins in verse 21 with this directive:

> *Submit to **one another** out of reverence for Christ* (emphasis mine).

It continues with more instruction:

> *Wives, submit yourselves to your own husbands as you do to the Lord. For the husband is the head of the wife as Christ is the head of the church, his body, of which he is the Savior. Now as the church submits to Christ, so also wives should submit to their husbands in everything (5:22-24).*

Perhaps your former partner focused on just these three verses, failing to apply the next eight verses to himself. Note as you read this passage that it is calling for *mutual* submission:

*Husbands, love your wives, just as Christ loved the church and **gave himself up for her** to make her holy, cleansing her by the washing with water through the word, and to present her to himself as a radiant church, without stain or wrinkle or any other blemish, but holy and blameless. In this same way, husbands ought to love their wives as their own bodies. He who loves his wife loves himself. After all, no one ever hated their own body, but **they feed and care for their body**, just as Christ does the church—for we are members of his body. "For this reason a man will leave his father and mother and be united to his wife, and the two will become one flesh." This is a profound mystery—but I am talking about Christ and the church (5:25-32; emphasis mine).*

A husband who follows these eight verses is submitting his life and will to the Lord, but he is also submitting to his wife. If he gives himself up for her, and cares for her as he does his own body, he is submitting his needs to hers. Paul sums up his discussion of Christian submission in marriage:

However, each one of you also must love his wife as he loves himself, and the wife must respect her husband (v. 33).

John Piper, a renowned preacher, says the husband's position as the leader in the home does not give him the right to command and control his wife.[99] It's a responsibility of the husband to love like Christ: to lay down his life for his wife through servant leadership. And the submission of the wife is not meant to be slavish or coerced or cowering. That's not the way Christ wants the church to respond to His leadership: He wants it to be free and willing and glad and refining and strengthening. In the same way that the church has free will and the Lord desires for the church to choose to follow Him, so also as wives we have free will to choose to follow our husbands—and this also is God's desire. Again, love is a choice.

In other words, Ephesians 5 is meant to do two things: to guard against the abuses of the husband's leadership by telling husbands to love like Jesus; and to guard against the debasing of submission by telling wives to respond to their husbands the way the church does to Christ.

Another set of verses that have been used to describe submission in the Bible come from Genesis 2:18–23:

The Lord God said, "It is not good for the man to be alone. I will make a helper suitable for him.". . . So the LORD God caused the man to fall into a deep sleep; and while he was sleeping, he took one of the man's ribs and closed up the place with flesh. Then the Lord God made a woman from the rib he had taken out of the man, and he brought her to the man.

The man said, "This is now bone of my bones, and flesh of my flesh; she shall be called 'woman,' for she was taken out of man" (2:18, 21-23).

Biblical scholar Dr. Walter C. Kaiser says that the word translated in the NIV as *helper* (which is used in Genesis 2:18 and 2:20 to describe the woman) comes from the Hebrew word *ezer*, meaning "to rescue, to save," and/or possibly the word *gezer*, meaning "to be strong." Furthermore, the word translated as *suitable* in the NIV comes from the Hebrew word *kĕnegdÔ*, which means "corresponding to him" or "equal to him." Therefore, Kaiser's translation of the woman's position in the marriage is as "a *strong rescuer who is equal* to the man."[100]

Therefore, "suitable helper" does not connote a weaker, inferior, or subordinate position. Her role may be different, but she is not less valuable or somehow less important. I believe in the context of a loving marriage, God calls women to submit their lives and wills to that of their husbands. I believe God has placed the husband in the role of the leader of the home, and his wife's role is to help him to carry out whatever he feels he is being called to do by the Lord. This does not mean she must blindly do whatever he says without discussion. I believe the two are a team, and working together will be better than either of them working alone. However, in cases where there is disagreement, she should lovingly, kindly allow him to lead, and trust that God will use her submission for His purposes.

A husband who is not abusive will respond favorably to a woman who loves him, thinks about him, and gives herself up for him. On the other hand, a man who is abusive will "ask for"—really, demand—more and more obedience from his wife. This type of man will most likely not be won over by this behavior, but will feel entitled to this type of treatment and see it as another way he can control her. In their book *Boundaries* (first referenced in Chapter 2 of this book), Henry Cloud and John

> "Suitable helper" does not connote a weaker, inferior position. A wife's role may be different, but it is not less important.

Townsend write, "We have never seen a 'submission problem' that didn't have a controlling husband at its root."[101] I pray your new husband is not an abusive man, and the two of you will have a marriage like the one described in Ephesians 5—a marriage based on love and respect.

Other Concerns Due to the Abuse You've Experienced

Marrying after being abused presents a special set of problems, even if your new husband is a loving Christian man, you have spent lots of time healing before your marriage, and you both use wisdom while courting each other. Other problems may still arise. Here are some I experienced.

Early in my second marriage, I needed to unlearn a bad habit I had learned in my first, abusive marriage. I had grown used to holding in my thoughts, desires, and needs. I was often afraid to tell my new husband if I was upset with something he had done. I found myself silently stewing about things, just as I used to do with my first husband. This was a reasonable self-protection method with my first husband, who didn't care what I thought or felt. If I ever *did* tell him, he went into a rage or gave me the silent treatment, sometimes for a month at a time.

However, I had now married a completely different man. Holding in my thoughts was unwise. He wanted to know what I thought, what I needed. And I would tell him—eventually, anyway. In the meantime, I was miserable, and he felt a distance between us because I was angry, but wouldn't tell him why. Not only that, he couldn't understand why I waited so long to tell him what was bothering me. What a mess. Over a period of several years, I have learned to tell him my thoughts right away. We are both much happier.

Another issue we struggle with is that I have trouble receiving his anger, even if it is expressed in the mildest manner possible. When he is stressed about work, he sometimes gets short-tempered. If I ask him a question he thinks is unnecessary, he will sometimes answer me with a slight edge to his voice. I immediately think: *Why is he mad at me? He must not love me!* In reality, the edge to his voice usually has nothing to do with me. He is stressed, and this is how his stress comes out. We have had many conversations about this. I have learned to ask him what is going on the minute he does this, rather than getting hurt and holding it in for days.

Your reactions to your new husband and your previous abuse might look completely different than mine. Know you probably will struggle in some way. Don't be surprised. The struggle does not mean you married the wrong man, or you married too soon. You both will need to be patient, to persevere (1 Corinthians 13:7). Hopefully, you will have talked through many of these issues in your premarital counseling. Personally, I found I was unaware of the number of issues I would experience until we were married. If you find this to be true for your marriage, I recommend you seek counseling together so neither of you have to feel you are walking on eggshells. You both deserve to feel the freedom marriage provides to love with passion and abandon.

Learning to Set Boundaries

Many formerly abused women have trouble setting reasonable boundaries with their loved ones. I grew up in a home where my parents didn't give me permission to say no, nor did they allow opinions that differed from theirs. It was "their way or the highway." Perhaps you grew up in a similar home. Because of the way I was raised, I was an easy target for my first husband. Cloud and Townsend explain in their book that controlling people have a hard time looking past themselves, and they search for someone to take care of them. They gravitate toward someone with blurry boundaries, someone who will naturally take on too much responsibility in the relationship and won't complain about it. They say, "It's like the old joke about relationships: What happens when a rescuing, enabling person meets a controlling, insensitive person? Answer: They get married!" A compliant person looks for someone to fix. This keeps them saying yes, and neglecting their own needs. Who better to marry than a controlling, insensitive person? And a controlling person is looking for someone to keep them from having to take responsibility for their own lives. Who better than a compliant person?[102]

> Setting boundaries with others doesn't make you selfish. You will be able to give more to others when they really need you if you learn to put yourself first at the right times.

You are no longer in your former abusive relationship, and you may now be in a good, healthy marriage. So how do you begin to set reasonable boundaries with your new husband? It will take practice and courage. You will need to practice saying no when you don't want to do something. Sometimes your spouse will be upset with you, and you will need to accept his feelings without changing your answer. You will need to learn to choose to do what is best for you rather than him or your children. You won't do this all the time, and choosing yourself on occasion doesn't mean you've become selfish, but it will mean you value yourself as much as you value others. By putting yourself first when you need to, you will be able to give more to others when they really need you.

Here's how I set a boundary recently with my family. I have been having trouble finding time to write because of the demands of our busy family. I decided I needed to spend a week away to devote some undivided time to writing. Leaving during a busy time in our family's life was inconvenient to my husband and kids. While I was gone, they had to do many of the jobs I usually do for them. However, I was able to accomplish in five days what would normally take me eight to ten weeks to do at home. My husband supported me in this. Yes, I felt a bit guilty leaving just for "me," but it was so worth it.

What If Marriage Is Really Hard?

In their book, *The Meaning of Marriage,* Timothy and Kathy Keller describe the end of the honeymoon period of marriage, when you wake up and realize you have married a "stranger."[103] Suddenly, many of the traits you thought were so cute when you were dating and first married are not so cute. Your husband who seemed so laid back now appears to be disorganized and unreliable. Or, he used to appear so independent to you, and now you see he hates to make joint decisions and never wants to ask for help, and this drives you crazy. And guess what? At the same time, he is finding out some things about the stranger *he* married. You may be a perfectionist, with a tendency to look down on others, be harsh in your opinions, and also hard on yourself. Or, because of your former abuse, you may find it hard to tell him the truth about your feelings and you may hide parts of yourself from him. As a result, he has a difficult time knowing what you think and feel.

What now? This is the time to put love into action. You may have many days when you don't feel lovingly toward your new husband. Act lovingly anyway. Remember 1 Corinthians 13:7: *[Love] always protects, always trusts, always hopes, always perseveres.*

Now is the time to protect your love, trust in the Lord, hope for the future, and persevere. Presuming you have married a Christian, ask your

> When you marry, your spouse must become your most significant relationship.

husband to pray with you for your marriage. If he won't, you pray. God cares deeply about marriage. Marriage was His idea (Genesis 2:19-25). As it says in Ecclesiastes 4:12: *A cord of three strands is not quickly broken.* The three strands of your marriage are you, your husband, and God. Allow God into your marriage. He will walk beside you both.

Stepparenting Is Hard

While it's true God will walk beside you both during your marriage, marrying after abuse, especially if one or both of you already have children, is difficult. I adore my second husband, and cannot imagine life without him, but being a stepparent is unbelievably hard and, more often than not, really painful. However, if you put aside your needs for the needs of your stepchildren and love them with Jesus' love, you can be a huge blessing in their lives. They may in turn teach you things about yourself you never would have learned any other way. Yes, it is difficult to be a stepparent, but with God's help, you can bring beauty from the ashes of broken marriages through stepparenting.

Once you marry, your spouse must become your most significant human relationship. This is counterintuitive for most people. We parents love and want to protect our kids above all others, especially after they have lived through our abusive relationships. However, Genesis 2:24 clearly says:

> *That is why a man leaves his father and mother*
> *and is united to his wife, and they become one flesh.*
> *Adam and his wife were both naked, and they felt no shame.*

We are to be so united to our spouse that we become like one flesh; we can be naked with one another, both physically and emotionally, and feel no shame. Though we don't "leave" our children, in a sense they should take second chair in the family, just as they would have in your original marriage. Though they may feel hatred toward their new stepparent, their sense of security depends on your new marriage succeeding.

If your new marriage fails, they will have less faith in relationships and marriage. Also, you and your children may lose your home, along with possibly their school and their friends. Your new marriage won't succeed if you put your children before your husband. Therefore, you are doing the best for your kids when you put their stepparent before them. Of course, you still love them as much as you always did, but don't allow them to disrespect your new husband and drive a wedge between the two of you by their actions or poor behavior. Discipline them if they behave badly to him or his children. Don't side with them over your husband. If you do, you will all suffer—your kids, your husband, your marriage, and ultimately, you.

My husband and I have many children from our first marriages. They have all been hurt by the abuse they suffered, by divorce, and by the pain of living part-time with mom and part-time with dad. In addition, they now have a stepparent and stepsiblings. When they come to us with the anger and pain these situations have caused them, this is what we tell them: "Divorce is not God's best plan. God's best plan is for a first marriage to be healthy and happy. This didn't happen for us. We know you have been affected by our poor choices in the past. We are sorry for the pain our divorces and remarriage has caused you. At the same time, we hope to show you what a good marriage can look like. We believe God can redeem our past and bring something beautiful out of our poor choices. We love you and are here for you." We realize saying this doesn't relieve the pain they are feeling in the moment, but we hope it will help them look toward the future.

What Do You Do When There Are Problems?

You will have problems. This is true of any marriage, and especially true of a marriage after abuse. I highly recommend you and your husband read and do the exercises together in *The Seven Principles for Making Marriage Work*[104] by John Gottman. Many books on marriage suggest the only thing you need for a happy marriage is to learn to communicate with each other. Gottman has spent more than two decades researching what makes a good marriage, and he shares his research in a refreshing way.

Finally, if or when you have more serious marriage problems, I highly recommend you get a good counselor. See Chapter 6, where I describe the benefits of counseling, and also how to find a good counselor. I don't know how my second husband and I would have made it through the first few years of our marriage without a good counselor to help us wade through issues with our kids. If you used a counselor in your single days, you will want to choose someone new for marriage counseling. Otherwise, your husband may feel as if you and your counselor are ganging up on him. Start fresh with someone new if possible. (Ethical standards strongly recommend you choose a new therapist for couples work, and if you *do* stay with the same person for your work as a couple that you used for your individual counseling, you should not return to individual work with that therapist. The therapist needs to work with either the individual or the couple.) If your husband refuses to go and you believe you need counseling, go without him. Better that one of you gets good advice than neither of you.

Summary

Any marriage is difficult, but marriage after abuse is even more difficult. However, if you are both committed to the Lord and each other, and willing to be patient and persevere, your new marriage can be a blessing to you both. Your marriage can also bring you great healing, and bring honor to the Lord as others see you following His plan for marriage.

A Drink of Water for the Journey

"When over the years someone has seen you at your worst, and knows you with all your strengths and flaws, yet commits him- or herself to you wholly, it is a consummate experience. To be loved but not known is comforting but superficial. To be known and not loved is our greatest fear. But to be fully known and truly loved is, well, a lot like being loved by God. It is what we need more than anything. It liberates us from pretense, humbles us out of our self-righteousness, and fortifies us for any difficulty life can throw at us."

—Timothy Keller, *The Meaning of Marriage: Facing the Complexities of Commitment with the Wisdom of God*

1. Have you considered getting married because of any of the "poor reasons for getting married" listed in this chapter? Do you agree these are poor reasons for marriage?

2. Do you agree with the author that love is not a feeling but an action? Do you agree that a Christian should never marry a non-Christian?

3. If you were to marry an abuser, what steps would you take after realizing abuse is an unfortunate reality in your new marriage?

4. Do you believe a man's greatest need from his wife is to be respected? Have you experienced this?

5. Does the idea of submission in marriage frighten you? Has someone used this idea to hurt you in the past? Do you agree biblical submission as described in Ephesians 5 (by both partners) can be God's design for a beautiful marriage?

6. Do you have trouble setting boundaries with others, particularly your potential husband? Does the idea of setting boundaries with him frighten you? Do you believe telling him no means you are selfish? Is setting boundaries something you need to work on?

7. What do you and your future spouse think are appropriate roles and responsibilities for a stepparent? Do you think your marriage is strong enough to withstand the trials that might come with raising each other's children?

8. Do you agree that putting your new husband before your children is actually better for your children in the long run? If so, do you think you can do this?

CHAPTER 11

Look for the Good God Promises Will Come from Our Pain

In my faithfulness I will reward my people
and make an everlasting covenant with them.

—Isaiah 61:8

No one wants to suffer, but while we are on earth, we all will suffer in some way. We don't get to pick how or when we will suffer. Even Jesus suffered from evil and a cruel death. God can redeem our suffering, but we will still have scars. A ransomed slave still wears scars from being chained and beaten. Even Jesus' resurrected body had scars in his hands from the nails that held Him to the cross. Our scars won't prevent us from being useful to God, just as Jesus' scars didn't prevent Him from being our savior.

I have been told the Lord never wastes a painful experience in our lives.

And we know that in all things God works for the good of those who love
him, who have been called according to his purpose (Romans 8:28).

This is one of the most well-known verses in the Bible. But when you are hurting, does hearing it make you angry? If so, it's understandable. You have been through a terrible experience. It might have lasted two months or forty years. The pieces of your broken life are lying all around you. How can God possibly use this experience for your *good*? He does so by:

1. Teaching you to trust Him more.

2. Giving you opportunities to glorify Him.

3. Helping you heal by serving others.

4. Helping you work to prevent domestic violence in society.

Learning to Trust God

God can use your abuse to teach you to trust Him, just as He taught Corrie ten Boom. Corrie was a Christian in Holland whose family hid Jews from the Nazis during World War II. The Nazis caught them and sent her family to concentration camps, where her father and sister died. Her story became famous in the book and movie *The Hiding Place*.[105]

After the war, Corrie traveled the United States sharing her story. She often showed the back side of a tapestry as an object lesson. On the back of any tapestry is a mass of threads that make no pattern. The weaver uses both light and dark threads of many colors to weave it. Corrie would explain that the dark threads are needed to create the beauty, and the same is true with our lives. We learn and grow more when we are in our "dark valley" times. This is when we learn to trust God. When our lives improve, we often feel like we need Him less.

> God can use your abuse for good by:
> - teaching you to trust Him more
> - giving you opportunities to glorify Him
> - helping you heal by serving others
> - helping you prevent domestic violence in society

After Corrie explained about the dark and light threads used in a tapestry, she would turn it over and show the beauty on the other side. So it is in our lives. God is weaving the tapestry of your life and mine. We won't know what the finished product looks like until God finishes weaving the tapestry and we are with Him in Heaven.

Learning to Trust God with the Pain You've Experienced

You may struggle with trusting God because you feel He didn't protect you from the abuse you've suffered when He could have. This story may help. Andrew Murray was a beloved pastor and writer in England in the late 1800s. One morning, a woman came to his home in desperate trou-

> Just as a weaver must use dark threads to make a tapestry beautiful, the dark times in our lives make our lives more beautiful when we learn to trust God.

ble, asking for his advice. Andrew handed her a writing he had penned to himself during a period when he was suffering terrible pain. It read:

In times of trouble, say, 'First, He brought me here. It is by His will I am in this straight place; in that I will rest.' Next, 'He will keep me here in His love, and give me grace in this trial to behave as His child.' Then say, 'He will make the trial a blessing, teaching me lessons He intends me to learn, and working in me the grace He means to bestow.' And last, say, 'In His good time He can bring me out again. How and when, He knows.' Therefore, say, 'I am here (1) by God's appointment, (2) in His keeping, (3) under His training, (4) for His time.'[106]

I would internalize Murray's words for myself in this way:

"I am here, working on healing from my abuse, because God allowed this in my life. He is here with me, and will never leave me nor forsake me. While I am here, I will learn what He wants me to learn and grow in whatever way He wants me to grow. When I've learned the lessons He means for me to learn, He will change my situation by taking away my pain, or by bringing me home to be with Him."

Learning to Trust God with the Whys

Perhaps you feel as if you trusted God to save you when you were being abused, and he refused. Now you are left wondering *why*? In *Calm My Anxious Heart*, Linda Dillow uses Habakkuk as an example of an Old Testament prophet who trusted God when he couldn't understand why God was doing what He did.[107]

Habakkuk comes to God asking why He allowed evil and injustice to continue in Judah. The Lord answers that He indeed has a plan, but it isn't what Habakkuk expects. God's answer for dealing with Judah's sin is to allow the Babylonians to sweep over Judah and destroy it.

Habakkuk couldn't believe the answer! Why would God use the Babylonians, who are even more wicked than the Judeans, to punish His people? This made no sense! It would only make things worse, Habakkuk reasoned. He appealed to God's character—His holiness and purity—and asked God *why*.

Then Habakkuk stood on the ramparts and waited for God to answer. God affirmed that the Babylonians were coming, but He didn't explain the why. But He did tell Habakkuk this:

> . . . *the righteous will live by his faith (Habakkuk 2:4, ESV).*

How frustrating! Surely God should explain Himself to Habakkuk! Don't we often wish God would tell us why He allows something to happen in our lives? Sometimes we understand why, but most often we don't. God is God, and He doesn't need to explain Himself. If we could fully understand God, He wouldn't be God. When He doesn't tell us *why*, we feel as if we are looking at the back side of a tapestry. We will not get to see the front until we are in Heaven.

> Even though God doesn't explain His actions, Habakkuk chooses to respond with a declaration of faith.

Even though Habakkuk is afraid, and still doesn't know why, he chooses to stand and wait patiently. Even though his body is rebelling to the point that decay is creeping into his bones, Habakkuk makes a beautiful declaration of faith:

> *Though the fig tree does not bud*
> *and there are no grapes on the vines,*
> *though the olive crop fails*
> *and the fields produce no food,*
> *though there are no sheep in the pen*
> *and no cattle in the stalls,*
> *yet I will rejoice in the Lord,*
> *I will be joyful in God my Savior.*
> *The Sovereign Lord is my strength;*
> *he makes my feet like the feet of a deer,*
> *he enables me to tread on the heights.*
> *(Habakkuk 3:17-19)*

Habakkuk was honest about his doubts in God, yet made a decision to wait on God and trust in Him even in the dark times—ultimately, to live by faith.

I've written my own version of this proclamation.

> *Though my husband abused me,*

though I am now divorced and remarried,
though I must share my kids with my ex, and am now a stepmother,
yet I will rejoice in the Lord. I will be joyful in God my savior.
The Sovereign Lord is my strength;
He helps me through each day,
and walks me through the muck of my life.

Can you write your own version of Habakkuk's proclamation?

Turning Abuse into Opportunities to Glorify God

In addition to causing you to trust God more, your abuse can give you more opportunities to glorify Him. When I was going through my divorce, my mentor Mary handed me a letter written by Pastor John Piper. At that time, the courts were giving my soon-to-be ex-husband more and more time with our children and less and less restrictions from harassing me. I was beside myself. Mary thought Dr. Piper's letter would help me see my circumstances from God's perspective, and it did. Piper wrote the letter on the eve of his prostate surgery, describing how a person with cancer would waste their pain. Then he gave ideas how *not* to do that.[108] The same concepts apply to a person who has been a victim of domestic violence.

> According to John Piper, your pain should:
>
> - remind you how much you need God
> - make you realize how much you need others
> - encourage you to point others to Jesus

You will waste your pain if you spend too much time reading about domestic violence and not enough time reading about the Lord.

It isn't wrong to learn about domestic violence. Some knowledge can help you move into your future. But your pain should point you toward your need for God. The apostle Paul wrote:

I press on to take hold of that for which Christ Jesus took hold of me . . .
Forgetting what is behind and straining toward what is ahead, I press on
toward the goal to win the prize for which God has called me heavenward
in Christ Jesus (Philippians 3:12-14).

Pressing on in this way will help you be like:

> *. . . a tree planted by streams of water,*
> *which yields its fruit in season*
> *and whose leaf does not wither—*
> *whatever [you] do prospers (Psalm 1:3).*

You will waste your pain if it drives you to be alone instead of reaching out to God's people.

> *And let us consider how we may spur one another on toward love and good deeds, not giving up meeting together, as some are in the habit of doing, but encouraging one another (Hebrews 10:24, 25).*

You may be tempted to retreat into yourself when you are in pain. But you need your brothers and sisters in Christ now more than ever. This is the time you can lean on them, and they can encourage you. Sometime in the future, you can encourage others.

You will waste your pain if you don't use it to further God's kingdom.

Christians are never anywhere by accident. God places you where He does on purpose. You may be able to share the message of Jesus with a fellow victim at the women's shelter. You might impress your non-Christian judge with your lack of bitterness toward your ex-husband, and she will know this is because you are a Christian. Remember, Jesus told us that we would be persecuted:

> *". . . they will seize you and persecute you. They will hand you over to synagogues and put you in prison, and you will be brought before kings and governors, and all on account of my name. And so you will bear testimony to me" (Luke 21:12, 13).*

When you are in pain, you will not be alone. Jesus will give you the help you need.

> *And my God will meet all your needs according to the riches of his glory in Christ Jesus (Philippians 4:19).*

Therefore, don't waste your pain. Use it as an opportunity to point others to Jesus.

Healing Yourself By Serving Others

And you will be called priests of the Lord,
you will be named ministers of our God.

—Isaiah 61:6

When you focus on all the negative things that have happened in your life, you are apt to feel isolated, helpless, depressed. Looking outside yourself to help others allows you to see your life from a different perspective. First, having somewhere to go regularly where people are counting on you will get you out of the house. Being with others doing something you enjoy will lift your spirits; you will no longer feel isolated because you will be working with others. Your fellow volunteers might become great friends. Second, the people you are helping may see you as someone they can trust, which will make you feel less helpless and more capable. You will begin to see gifts and attributes in yourself you never knew you had, or you never valued—but other people do. Third, because you are no longer isolated, and you are beginning to feel better about yourself, your depression will ease. You will find your self-esteem growing over time.

> Serving others will help you move from feeling:
>
> • isolated to . . . included
> • helpless to . . . capable
> • depressed to . . . valued

How do you find a volunteer job to help serve others and grow your self-esteem at the same time? Begin by listing everything you are interested in. Do you love children? You might begin by volunteering to hold babies in your church nursery once a month. Once your confidence builds, you might become a Sunday school teacher. Later, you might move on to become a youth leader or your church's children's director. Start small; God will provide the right avenues.

Do you have a heart for the poor? You and your children might volunteer to serve a dinner at your local rescue mission. You may like this, and decide to do this monthly or weekly. Over time, you might move into a full-time position there. Do you love the elderly? Many older people in nursing homes have no one to visit them. You and your kids could meet a resident and visit weekly, becoming a ray of sunshine to him or her. Are

Look for the Good God Promises Will Come from Our Pain

you good with languages? You might volunteer to teach an English as a Second Language (ESL) course at your local community college. Do you enjoy art? Many elementary schools no longer have the funds to pay an art teacher, and they seek volunteers to provide their art classes. You don't need to be a great artist to do this, just someone who will put in the time and love students.

People you might help:

- children
- the poor
- the elderly
- immigrants
- students

Preventing Domestic Violence in Society

If you allow Him, the Lord can use your experiences to teach you to trust and glorify Him and begin to help others. In addition, you can use your experiences to prevent domestic violence in society by:

- helping other women who are being abused
- helping your church become more knowledgeable about domestic violence
- helping children who are being abused
- working to prevent domestic violence in society at large.

Help Other Women Who Are Being Abused

You can help other women to accept the comfort of the Lord that you received.

Praise be to the God and Father of our Lord Jesus Christ, the Father of compassion and the God of all comfort, who comforts us in all our troubles, so that we can comfort those in any trouble with the comfort we ourselves have received from God (2 Corinthians 1:3, 4).

Here are two examples from my life. Shortly after I separated from my husband, the Lord gave me several opportunities to minister to other abused women. I was surprised how many of these women were people I had known for years, but never knew they were being abused. In one case, a friend of mine asked for prayer for her marriage in a small group meeting. Though she made no mention of abuse, the Lord gave me intuition she might be an abused woman. I invited her to my home and began telling her about the abuse I had experienced in my first mar-

212

riage. She quickly opened up and told me her husband was emotionally abusing her. I gave her books to read about domestic violence as well as phone numbers for the National Domestic Hotline and shelters nearby.

Another friend (I will call her Jane) had been praying for a year that someone would step in and help her. One day, I saw her four-year-old child punch his baby sister in the face. When I invited her to lunch, she told me her husband had been emotionally abusive toward her and using harsh physical punishment with their children for quite a while. She wasn't frightened of him at that time, however. I gave her the same books on domestic violence and the same phone numbers I had given my other friend.

> Your past abuse could give you a strong intuition that another woman is experiencing abuse, and may increase your compassion for her and her children.

Things seemed to improve for a few months in Jane's home, which was probably a honeymoon stage in the abuse cycle. I hadn't talked to her for several weeks when I received a phone call from her. Jane told me her husband had tried to strangle her while she was holding their one-year-old baby. Because I had been willing to open up and share with her, Jane had the courage to call the police and have him arrested, then removed from their home. I thank the Lord I was able to help her in this way. I cannot imagine how I would have felt if I hadn't spoken to her.

Each time I spoke with an abused woman, I asked her not to mention my name to her husband. Because abuse goes in cycles, a woman may not leave her husband for many years, if ever. When her husband is in a honeymoon stage, she might tell him she had talked with someone, which could put that someone—me, in this case—in danger. I had to rely on the Lord to protect me, as He had during my marriage.

After recovering from your own abuse, you may find you will be able to help other women suffering from domestic violence. Your experiences could give you a strong intuition when another woman is in pain and may increase your compassion for her and her children. Many crisis centers offer free training for those who wish to become domestic violence advocates. You might find a rewarding career in this way, or you might want to volunteer for a domestic violence hotline or in a women's shelter. I encourage you to reach out and help other women in any way you can. You will be blessed, and this work will help you bring beauty out of the ashes of your painful experience (Isaiah 61:3).

Help Your Church Become More Knowledgeable About Domestic Violence

The Lord can also use you to help your church become more knowledgeable about domestic violence. Hopefully, your church supported you when you were living with your abuser. If that was not your experience, you can be a vehicle of education and change. Be assured other women in your church are being abused right now.

How God redeemed the pain my church caused me

When I was married to my abuser, I asked my pastor for help. Unfortunately, he didn't understand the dynamics of domestic violence. Because my abuse was mostly emotional, he didn't hold my husband accountable for his actions. My husband told him everything was fine between us, and our pastor believed him. After a while, I gave up trying to seek help from the church. When I finally was afraid for my life, I got a restraining order and had my husband removed from our house.

Our pastor then sent me a letter telling me I had no biblical right to divorce. He said I should work toward reconciling with my husband, and if I was unwilling to, I should step down from my leadership positions in the church.

I have rarely been so angry in my life. I thought my pastor had betrayed me, and left me to hang in the wind, with no one to protect me. Asking me to reconcile with my husband was the final blow. I remained in the church for the sake of my kids, but I avoided my pastor. If I saw him coming down the hall, I would turn and walk the other way.

About a year after I received the restraining order, I began studying Jeff Rosenau's book *Building Bridges Not Walls: Learning to Dialogue in the Spirit of Christ*.[109] Rosenau believes people with radically different views on a topic can work with each other to resolve problems, and unbelievers may even be drawn to Christ through a Holy Spirit-led dialogue.

As I was reading this book, I started praying about my relationship with my pastor. The Lord convicted me I should see if my pastor was willing to dialogue with me in the Spirit of Christ. I sent him an email asking if he'd be willing to meet with me to discuss the church's views on domestic violence and how it could help other victims. He agreed.

When we met, after a few minutes of small talk, I asked if we could pray together; he agreed. Next, I asked if I had done or said anything that had hurt him. This question obviously surprised him. He thought for a moment, groped for words, thought some more, and finally answered, "No." I am sure people don't often start conversations with their pastors in that way!

Finally, he said, "There are some things I would have done differently, though." We then had a very friendly, respectful conversation. I was able to humbly share with him the ways I felt hurt and abandoned by the church, and what I would like to see changed. After listening, he said, "So, your vision for the church is . . ." I thought that was an excellent way of describing what I was feeling. I *did* have a vision for the church. My vision was that caring people who were knowledgeable about domestic violence would come alongside couples experiencing domestic violence, hold the abusers accountable, and assist victims who needed help.

He was, in theory, willing to do this, though he never got around to following through with learning more about domestic violence and implementing the changes I hoped for. I was disappointed, but the Lord blessed me through my willingness to meet with my pastor and dialogue with him in the Spirit of Christ. First, God repaired our relationship. I no longer felt the need to walk in the other direction when I saw my pastor coming down the hall! Even more important, the Lord healed my heart and allowed me to completely forgive my pastor. Praise Him!

> Every church has abuse victims. Most churches could improve their knowledge of domestic violence and responses to these victims. You could become an agent of change for your church.

Later I moved to another church. At this church I was able to work with the pastor to define domestic violence policies for the church that were ratified by the elders. After I was trained to be a domestic violence advocate, I was able to act as the advocate for the church and train our leadership and congregation about domestic violence.

Other ways to educate your church

Even if you don't train to be a domestic violence advocate, you can help your church become more knowledgeable about domestic violence by:

- giving your pastor and elders books on domestic violence to read.[110] Ask them if they will place the books in the church lobby or library.

- asking your pastor if you can bring in advocates from your local women's crisis center to train the congregation about domestic violence.

- working with your local missions team to have a domestic violence awareness day in October each year.

- being creative!

Is it OK to change churches?

I have a final note to share about working with your church. Depending on what the circumstances are, and how much the church supported or did not support you, you may decide you should move to another church. I chose to remain at my church for a while for the sake of my teenaged children, who were brought up there. Later, I moved on. Seek the Lord's guidance for what is best. The important thing is not to lose your relationship with Him. Be sure you get support from the body of Christ as you seek healing.

Help Children Who Are Being Abused

One of the best ways to prevent domestic violence from continuing in society is to support children who are living in homes with domestic violence. See Chapter 7 for ideas on how to help your own children heal from the abuse they have experienced or are continuing to experience.

What can you do to help children who live with domestic violence? The best thing for them is to support their mothers. The more help you give abused women, the better these mothers will be able to support their kids. Your might help women in the following ways:

- emotionally

- with education about domestic violence

- financially

- supporting your local women's crisis center

- with legal aid.

The best way to help abused children themselves is to give them as much unconditional love as you possibly can. You may meet these kids in a school or church setting, or in your neighborhood. They may be needy or combative. They may be poorly taken care of, and therefore dirty, have inadequate clothing, and may even be hungry. Or they may just be difficult to be around. Make every effort to demonstrate they are still lovable and worthy of your care and attention. Talk to them, and ask them if there is anything they want to tell you. If they tell you they are being abused, do not act on this knowledge unless you speak to their mother, and the mother and you believe action will make things better for her and her children. Read Chapter 7, where I describe calling Social Services for help; use God's wisdom before calling Social Services or the police. Children who are living in an abusive environment need to believe there are safe and consistent adults in their life. Be consistent in the way you approach them, how you speak to them, and the assistance you offer to them and their mother. Although you cannot stop the abuse, you can be a support and a reminder of God's goodness.

> To help a child who is being abused:
>
> • support his or her mother
> • show him or her unconditional love

Work to Change the Cycle of Abuse in Your Community and in Our Society

Half of all abusive men were abused as children. This means half of all abusers were not abused as children! Where did these men learn to be abusers? From the society we live in. They learned to devalue and abuse women from:

• peers

• other relatives besides parents

• television, movies, music

• pornography.

If we want to change the cycle of abuse in our society, we need to begin to change the culture around us that tacitly accepts violence against women. One way this happens is through victim blaming. When a woman is raped, she is often asked:

• "What were you wearing?"

• "Why were you out so late by yourself?"

- "Why didn't you fight harder?"

A victim of domestic violence is frequently asked:

- "Why did you marry him in the first place?"
- "Why didn't you leave sooner?"
- "Did you respect him as you should have?"

When we hear questions like these, we need to speak up and ask questions of our own. These include:

- "Why was the man out looking for someone to rape?"
- "Why did he think it was OK to use force to rape someone he didn't know (or did know)?"
- "Why did the abuser hide his true personality until after they were married?"
- "Why does he continually disrespect and frighten her?"

Another way to make a change in society is to use the media for good. Write articles and letters to the editor of your local newspaper. Post articles that stand against domestic violence to your Facebook, Twitter, and Pinterest accounts. Write letters of complaint, or call radio and television stations that air songs, movies, and shows that portray violence against women and children as funny or acceptable.

Use your voice and pen to lobby your local, state, and federal government. Become a member of a national or local domestic violence agency such as the National Coalition Against Domestic Violence.[111] NCADV frequently lobbies government agencies when bills dealing with domestic violence are being voted on in Congress. Lobby for justice to return to the family court system, either in your local court or on a national level.

Summary

Though you may struggle to understand why God allowed the abuse you've experienced, He can bring good from it. He will be able to bring you more good if you seek to trust Him through it, work to not waste your pain, begin to look outside yourself by helping others, and consider working to fight against domestic violence so others won't have to suffer as you have. If you do these things, you can move toward healing faster and more completely.

A Drink of Water for the Journey

Despite what some prosperity-gospel teachers claim, the Bible offers no guarantee that suffering will be removed, only that it will be redeemed—or, to use a more modern word, recycled. I take used and flattened aluminum cans to a redemption center in hopes that someone will make something useful out of them. I drop off an outdated computer knowing that a technician will remove the gold and rare earths and "redeem" them. In a parallel way, suffering too can be recycled as a contribution to an enriched life.

—PHILIP YANCEY IN *THE QUESTION THAT NEVER GOES AWAY*[112]

1. Do you believe God can use the pain you have experienced for good? Have you seen Him do this? If so, how?

2. Has your abuse caused you to trust God more or less? Why? Do you think you can learn to trust God even when you don't understand why?

3. Have you had the opportunity to serve others? Has that been healing for you? If you haven't yet tried this, what types of people or causes might you be interested in volunteering for?

4. Have you helped another abuse victim? What was that experience like?

5. Did your church support you as you went through the pain of being a domestic violence victim? Whether yes or no, would you be willing to help educate its leaders and members about domestic violence in an effort to help other victims in the future?

6. Do you know any children who you suspect are being abused? What are the best ways you can help those children?

7. Are you willing to stand up against our culture, one that tacitly accepts violence against women and children? If so, how can you do this?

EPILOGUE

You may feel you will never be healed. I feel the same at times. I get triggered even now by my stepkids, by people I minister with, by people in my church. Though I have had many years of counseling, I still get discouraged at times. Things can get really discouraging if we allow ourselves to think *God can't use me until I am completely healed.* This is a lie from Satan. There is no one on earth who is perfect, who doesn't have some pain from their past, or some sin they struggle with. Please remember: God uses us in spite of or even because of our imperfections. Even the apostle Paul got discouraged and asked God to take away the "thorn in my flesh." However, God said no. He told Paul: *"My grace is sufficient for you, for my power is made perfect in weakness"* (2 Corinthians 12:9).

If the apostle Paul struggled with uncertainty, I am in good company. Here is an allegory that helps me:

Imagine you were once a beautiful ceramic jar, perfect and whole. If someone were to put a small lamp inside the perfect jar, how much light would shine out? Only a little bit, from the opening at the top. Now, picture the jar broken and shattered into many pieces. This is a picture of our lives broken by the abuse we have suffered. God can take the many broken pieces of our lives and glue them back together. However, the jar will no longer be perfect. It will now have holes in it where small pieces of ceramic were shattered or lost. It doesn't look perfect on the outside any longer. Yet, what happens when the same small lamp is placed inside the broken ceramic jar? Light can now pour out through the holes where the broken places are.

This is an allegory of our lives if we give them to God for healing. The light represents God and His wisdom and joy. We can share this light with others who experience the same pain we have experienced. I have empathy for other abuse victims and survivors (and even other stepparents) I never would have had if I had never walked in their shoes. I can be more of a help to them because of my brokenness, not in spite of it.

* * * * *

I have mentioned many times how difficult I find being a stepmother. At the beginning of my second marriage, I struggled most with my stepson. He was just beginning high school and was going through what I assumed was a typical teen rebellion period. We found out later he was struggling with much more than that.

I remember many arguments we had, and some epic punishments we gave him. One argument involved him dyeing his hair blue in our bathroom (after we asked him not to). He got blue dye on our walls, ceiling, and carpet. We assigned him a long list of chores as a consequence, which made him furious. He refused to do them.

As time passed, he found subtle ways to hurt me. I would spend lots of time and energy making dinner for the family. We would all sit down at the table, pray together, and everyone but this son would begin eating. After a few minutes, he would get up from the table and quietly make himself a sandwich that he would eat at the counter. Those first couple of years were quite painful.

As he neared high school graduation, we went with him for family counseling. He and his dad had some difficult talks, and I sat on the far side of the couch trying not to cry. He decided to move back to his mother's house full-time for a while, which broke my heart. In a few weeks, he called to ask if he could move back, and we said yes.

Our relationship took a 180-degree turn after that. He slowly began talking to me, telling me what was on his heart. He went off to college in another state and we all missed him. When he returned for Christmas, he was more mature and desired to spend time with us. The following summer, our relationship deepened. I began to see a young man emerge.

Recently, I received the kind of phone call every mother dreams of receiving. He called and we chatted for a while. Then he told me, "A friend of mine asked me who was the most significant person in my life, and I said it was you." Then he started to cry! I had to sit down; I was so blown away. I told him I loved him, and he was my son. All of this had been quite the miracle. He said he believed that going through all this together made us closer in the long run.

When we hung up, I sat there stunned. A verse (Proverbs 31:28) came to me:

Her children arise and call her blessed.

Praise you, Jesus! You really do bring beauty out of ashes.

If you have enjoyed this book, please bless me by giving it a review on one or more internet retailers or Goodreads.com.

—CAROLINE ABBOTT

APPENDIX A: HOW TO USE *A JOURNEY TO HEALING* AS A GROUP STUDY GUIDE

This book was prepared with both individual use and small group study in mind. The chapters are written for close personal use, but the questions at the end of each chapter—A Drink of Water for the Journey—can easily be used by small groups.

Here are my suggestions for how to use *A Journey to Healing After Emotional Abuse* as a small group guide.

- **First, plan for groups of four to no more than eight women.** If the group is large, you might occasionally break into groups of two or three for deeper sharing.

- **Commit to goals for your group.** Ask the women their thoughts and goals. Discuss the level of confidentiality of the group, when confidentiality might not apply if there are safety concerns, whether the group will accept new members once it begins, how the group will handle conflict. Combine thoughts and work together so that everyone feels invested. Don't have one person set the entire agenda. That said . . .

- **Choose a group leader.** Someone needs to facilitate and direct. But that person should have a gentle hand in doing so and needs to make sure everyone is heard.

  Perhaps a licensed counselor or certified domestic violence advocate is available in your area or right in your group. If not, don't worry, it need not be a professional. Simply search for a natural leader.

- **Find a comfortable time and place.** Why "comfortable"? Going through this journey and talking about it is difficult enough! So, your setting . . . could be a coffee shop, sure, but you will be sharing about very intense topics, and that would be a very public setting. How about a meeting room at your local library or church, or in someone's home? Consider all the needs. Next, set a weekly time that works for all. (For instance, don't make it 6:30 a.m. if women in the group have young children at home.)

Commit to a weekly time as much as possible. I find that meeting only twice per month allows momentum to be lost.

- **Have each woman read a chapter each week, then come together for discussion.** This way, the book can be finished in eleven weeks. Or, you might like to make it twelve weeks, allowing the women to get to know each other the first week. If time is short, to make it an even ten weeks, you can combine weeks on two chapters that seem shorter.

- **Have the leader briefly summarize the chapter the first week.** After that, the members can take turns. (The key is *briefly*. The leader should not take 45 minutes to go over the chapter!) This will help anyone who has not had a chance to read the chapter during the week. Yes, the goal would be for all to read it, but you don't want to be too legalistic about it—this might drive women away.

- **Work through the questions provided in the Drink of Water section.** Give rough parameters of times for responses . . . one woman shouldn't take, say, twelve minutes to answer a question—but at the same time be flexible. Seek to work through the entire question set, but don't be upset if you cannot get to a question or two: quality is more important than quantity!

- **Try creative ideas!** Perhaps one member would like to do a dramatic reading of a poem or scriptural passage in a chapter, or write her own poem or letter to share.

- **Get everyone involved—in some way.** In group dynamics, one or two people often dominate, and a handful are too intimidated to speak much at all. Be gentle, but *work hard to get past this sort of group-dynamic inertia.* Get everyone involved!

- **Be flexible, be sensitive to each others' pain, and take every comment and thought seriously.** And one last thing, and it is possible with such a group, even with these topics: have fun!

Blessings, and may this book help all of you along your journey to healing.

—CAROLINE ABBOTT

APPENDIX B: TYPES OF ABUSE

Physical Abuse[113]
- Pushing, slapping, punching, biting, kicking, or strangling
- Throwing or otherwise destroying valued objects
- Harming children or pets
- Hair pulling
- Restraining or trapping
- Forcing you to leave your home
- Using a weapon to threaten or hurt you
- Driving recklessly
- Abandoning you in a dangerous or unfamiliar place
- Preventing you from calling police or seeking medical attention

Sexual Abuse
- Views women as objects and believes in rigid gender roles
- Insults you in sexual ways or calls you sexual names
- Has ever forced or manipulated you into having sex
- Held you down during sex
- Demanded sex when you were sick, tired, or after beating you
- Hurt you with weapons or objects during sex
- Involved other people in sexual activities with you
- Withholds sex from you
- Forces you to become pregnant, get an abortion, or kills your fetus

Verbal, Emotional, or Psychological Abuse
- Controls what you do, read, think, say, where you go, who you see
- Expects you to ask permission, treats you like a servant
- Calls you names, insults you, or continually criticizes you
- Humiliates you in any way
- Does not trust you and acts jealous or possessive
- Tries to isolate you from family or friends

- Makes you think you are crazy; plays mind games with you (identified as *gaslighting* in Chapter 1)
- Intimidates you with looks, actions, and gestures
- Punishes you by withholding affection
- Threatens to kill himself
- Threatens to hurt you, the children, your family, or your pets
- Uses the children against you
- Blames his abuse on you, or claims it never happened

Financial Abuse

- Keeps you from getting or keeping a job, or takes your money
- Controls finances, refuses to work (for the home or outside the home)
- Gives you an allowance, or refuses to share money

Spiritual Abuse

- Twists or distorts Scripture to control you or make you feel guilty, or to prevent you from leaving him

APPENDIX C: RESOURCES

Below you will find a wide collection of books, pamphlets, websites, and organizations. These resources can offer you support, guidance, and inspiration as you continue your journey to healing. They are arranged by topic.

ABUSE

The author's website: www.carolineabbott.com—Caroline provides many articles on abuse and healing.

For emergency phone numbers for countries around the world: http://www.911dispatch.com/911/911_world.html.

Go to DomesticShelters.org to find your nearest domestic violence shelter or crisis center (in the USA): www.domesticshelters.org.

National Domestic Violence Hotline: 1-800-799-SAFE (7233) or 1-800-787-3224 (TTY); www.thehotline.org (in the USA).

National Coalition Against Domestic Violence: http://www.ncadv.org

Lundy Bancroft, *Why Does He DO That? Inside the Minds of Angry and Controlling Men* (New York, NY: Berkley Books, 2002).

Patricia Evans, *The Verbally Abusive Relationship, How to Recognize It and How to Respond* (Avon, MA: Adams Media Corporation, 1996).

TO FURTHER YOUR CHRISTIAN WALK/FORGIVENESS

K-LOVE radio station has pastors on call 24 hours a day: http://www.klove.com/; 1-800-525-LOVE (5683).

Neil T. Anderson, *The Bondage Breaker: Overcoming Negative Thoughts Irrational Feelings Habitual Sins* (Eugene, OR: Harvest House Publishers, 2006).

Linda Dillow, *Calm My Anxious Heart, A Woman's Guide to Finding Contentment* (Colorado Springs: NavPress, 1998).

Jeff Rosenau, *Building Bridges Not Walls, Learning to Dialogue in the Spirit of Christ* (Colorado Springs, CO: NavPress, 2003). Note, this book has been rewritten, and is now called *When Christians Act like Christians: God's Call to Christlike Civility* (Centennial, CO: Jeff Rosenau, 2010). http://www.christlike-dialogue.org/small-group-study/when-christians-act-christians/.

Philip Yancey, *The Question that Never Goes Away: What is God Up to in a World of Such Tragedy and Pain?* (London, England: Hodder and Stoughton, 2013).

Bill Elliff with Tim Grissom, *Forgiveness, Healing the Harbored Hurts of Your Heart* (North Little Rock, AR: Summit Church, 1998).

LEARNING TO SET BOUNDARIES

Dr. Henry Cloud and Dr. John Townsend, *Boundaries, When to Say Yes When to Say No to Take Control of Your Life* (Grand Rapids, MI: Zondervan, 1992).

Cloud-Townsend Resources, 3176 Pullman Ave, # 104, Costa Mesa, CA 92626, 800-676-HOPE (4673); www.cloudtownsend.com .

COUNSELING and PSYCHOLOGY

American Psychiatric Association, *Diagnostic and Statistical Manual of Mental Disorders* (5th ed.) (American Psychiatric Association, 2013).

EMDR Institute, Inc., "What is EMDR?" http://www.emdr.com/general-information/what-is-emdr/what-is-emdr.html .

FIGHTING FOR CUSTODY OF YOUR CHILDREN

Caroline Abbott, "Hope for the Family Court System," May 2014, http://www.carolineabbott.com/2014/05/hope-for-the-family-court-system/.

Lundy Bancroft, *When Dad Hurts Mom: Helping Your Children Heal the Wounds of Witnessing Abuse* (New York, NY: Berkley Books, 2004).

Johnston, Walters, & Olesen, "Is it Alienating Parenting, Role Reversal or Child Abuse? A Study of Children's Rejection of a Parent in Child Custody Disputes," The Hayworth Press, 2005, https://www.ncjrs.gov/App/publications/abstract.aspx?ID=234543 .

Daniel G. Saunders, Ph.D., Kathleen C. Faller, Ph.D., Richard M. Tolman, Ph.D., "Child Custody Evaluators' Beliefs About Domestic Abuse Allegations: Their Relationship to Evaluator Demographics, Background, Domestic Violence Knowledge and Custody-Visitation Recommendations" https://www.ncjrs.gov/pdffiles1/nij/grants/238891.pdf .

DATING and BEING SINGLE

Emily Avagliano, *Dating After Trauma: How to Find the Love of Your Life After Experiencing an Abusive Relationship, Rape or Sexual Abuse* (USA: Bad Kitty Print Shoppe, 2013).

Joshua Harris, *Boy Meets Girl: Say Hello to Courtship* (Colorado Springs, CO: Multnomah Publishers, 2005).

Joshua Harris, *I Kissed Dating Goodbye* (Sisters, OR: Multnomah, 2003).

Kate McVeigh, *Single and Loving It, Living Life to the Fullest* (Tulsa: Harrison House, 2003).

THE BIBLE'S STANCE ON DIVORCE and REMARRIAGE

Jay Adams, *Marriage, Divorce, and Remarriage in the Bible: A Fresh Look at What Scripture Teaches* (Grand Rapids, MI: Zondervan, 1980).

Jeff Crippen and Anna Wood, *A Cry for Justice: How the Evil of Domestic Abuse Hides in Your Church* (USA: Calvary Press Publishing, 2012).

Herb Vander Lugt, "God's Protection of Women, When Abuse is Worse Than Divorce" (Grand Rapids, MI: RBC Ministries, 2005).

HEALING AFTER ABUSE

Meg Kennedy Dugan, M.A., and Roger R. Hock, Ph.D., *It's My Life Now – Starting Over After an Abusive Relationship or Domestic Violence* (New York and London: Routledge, 2000).

Brian F. Martin, *Invincible: The 10 Lies You Learn Growing Up with Domestic Violence and the Truths to Set You Free* (New York, NY: Perigee, 2014).

Karyl McBride, Ph.D., *Will I Ever Be Good Enough? Healing the Daughters of Narcissistic Mothers* (New York, NY: Free Press, 2008).

Eleanor D. Payson, M.S.W., *The Wizard of Oz and Other Narcissists: Coping with the One-Way Relationship in Work, Love and Family* (Royal Oak, MI: Julian Day Publications, 2002).

Steven R. Tracy, *Mending the Soul: Understanding and Healing Abuse* (Grand Rapids, MI: Zondervan, 2005).

MARRIAGE

Emerson Eggerichs, *Love & Respect: The Love She Most Desires, the Respect He Desperately Needs* (Nashville, TN: Thomas Nelson, 2004).

John M. Gottman, Ph.D, and Nan Silver, *The Seven Principles for Making Marriage Work: A Practical Guide from the Country's Foremost Relationship Expert* (New York, NY: Harmony Books, 2015).

Susan Heitler, Ph.D, Abigail Hirsch, MA, *The Power of Two Workbook: Communication Skills for a Strong and Loving Marriage* (Oakland, CA: New Harbinger Publications, Inc., 2003).

Timothy and Kathy Keller, *The Meaning of Marriage: Facing the Complexities of Commitment with the Wisdom of God* (New York, NY: Riverhead Books, 2013).

John Piper's sermon about submission, June 11, 1989, http://www.desiring-god.org/resource-library/sermons/husbands-who-love-like-christ-and-the-wives-who-submit-to-them .

RAISING YOUR KIDS

Scott Brown, *How to Negotiate with Kids . . . Even When You Think You Shouldn't: Seven Essential Skills to End Conflict and Bring More Joy into Your Family* (New York, NY: Penguin Putnam, Inc., 2004).

Dr. James Dobson, *Parenting Isn't for Cowards: The "You Can Do It" Guide for Hassled Parents* (Carol Stream, IL: Tyndale House Publishers, 2010).

Jim Weidmann and Kurt Bruner, *An Introduction to Family Nights: Family Night Tool Chest* (Colorado Springs, CO: Victor Books, 1997).

ENDNOTES

INTRODUCTION

[1] *Heal By Writing About Your Trauma* by Rochelle Melander. http://www.psychol-ogytoday.com/blog/stop-walking-eggshells/201211/heal-writing-about-your-trauma (accessed April 15, 2015).

CHAPTER ONE

[2] Advocates to End Domestic Violence, "Domestic Violence Facts—The Cycle of Violence," http://www.aedv.org/index.php/domestic-violence-facts (accessed January 29, 2013).

[3] Bridges Domestic and Sexual Violence Support, "What is Domestic Violence," http://www.bridgesnh.org/domestic_violence.php, accessed December 7, 2012. Adapted from Dr. Lenore Walker's "Cycle of Violence."

[4] Lundy Bancroft, *Why Does He DO That? Inside the Minds of Angry and Controlling Men* (New York, NY: Berkley Books, 2002).

[5] Meg Kennedy Dugan, M.A. and Roger R. Hock, Ph.D., *It's My Life Now – Starting Over After and Abusive Relationship or Domestic Violence* (New York and London:Routledge, 2000), 7.

CHAPTER TWO

[6] Dr. Henry Cloud and Dr. John Townsend, *Boundaries, When to Say Yes, When to Say No to Take Control of Your Life* (Grand Rapids, MI: Zondervan, 1992), 29, 33.

[7] See the author's website for Domestic Violence Hotline numbers in countries other than the United States: http://www.carolineabbott.com/get-help/.

[8] Danger Assessment http://www.dangerassessment.org (accessed 4/15/15).

[9] Discerning Your Danger Level – An App http://www.carolineabbott.com/2015/04/discerning-your-danger-level-an-app/ (accessed 4/16/15).

[10] You may not have to petition for a permanent order during the time you are working out the details of a legal separation, divorce, or child custody.

[11] For a great article on how pedophiles "groom" children and even entire families, see: "Is a Pedophile Targeting Your Child? Pedophiles Groom Both the Child and the Family" http://singlemum.com.au/features/child-abuser-risks-23102014-jayneen-sand-ers.html (accessed 4/15/15).

CHAPTER THREE

[12] American Psychiatric Association, *Diagnostic and Statistical Manual of Mental Disorders* (5th ed.) (American Psychiatric Association, 2013).

¹³ "Unraveling the Sun's Role in Depression More Evidence That Sunlight Affects Mood-Lifting Chemical in the Brain" http://www.webmd.com/mental-health/news/20021205/unraveling-suns-role-in-depression (accessed 4/16/15).

¹⁴ "Relaxation Techniques for Stress Relief" http://www.helpguide.org/articles/stress/relaxation-techniques-for-stress-relief.htm (accessed 4/16/15).

¹⁵ See Chapter 6 for more about triggers and what to do about them.

¹⁶ Check out this website for emergency phone numbers for countries around the world: http://www.911dispatch.com/911/911_world.html (accessed 4/16/15).

¹⁷ Meg Kennedy Dugan, M.A., and Roger R. Hock, Ph.D., *It's My Life Now – Starting Over After and Abusive Relationship or Domestic Violence* (New York and London: Routledge, 2000), 121.

¹⁸ Linda Dillow, *Calm My Anxious Heart, A Woman's Guide to Finding Contentment* (Colorado Springs, CO:NavPress, 1998).

¹⁹ Dillow, *Calm My Anxious Heart*, 154.

²⁰ Dillow, *Calm My Anxious Heart*, 155–156.

²¹ Jewish mourning traditions are presented: http://www.chabad.org/library/article_cdo/aid/281584/jewish/About-the-Shiva.htm (accessed 4/16/15).

²² Mourning traditions in the Civil War-era southern states of the United States: http://thecivilwarlady.webs.com/mourningcustomsandrituals.htm (accessed 4/16/15).

CHAPTER FOUR

²³ Steven R. Tracy, *Mending the Soul: Understanding and Healing Abuse* (Grand Rapids, MI: Zondervan, 2005), 173-174.

²⁴ Philip Yancey, *The Question that Never Goes Away: What is God Up to in a World of such Tragedy and Pain?*, (London, England: Hodder and Stoughton, 2013), 30.

²⁵ Yancey, *The Question that Never Goes Away*, 130.

²⁶ Yancey, *The Question that Never Goes Away*, 33.

²⁷ If you live somewhere other than the United States, envision the ruler at one of the shores of the continent you live on, and eternity on the opposite shore of that continent.

²⁸ Tracy, *Mending the Soul*, 74.

²⁹ Tracy, *Mending the Soul*, 75–76.

³⁰ Tracy, *Mending the Soul*, 84.

³¹ Tracy, *Mending the Soul*, 78.

³² Tracy, *Mending the Soul*, 87-88.

³³ Tracy, *Mending the Soul*, 89.

³⁴ See Psalm 17:13; 35:4-8, 24-26; 40:14; 69:19-28; 70:2, 83:13-17.

³⁵ Beth Moore, *Breaking Free: The Journey, The Stories* (Nashville, TN: LifeWay Press, 2009), 132.

CHAPTER FIVE

[36] UNICEF, "Behind Closed Doors: The Impact of Domestic Violence on Children," http://www.unicef.org/protection/files/BehindClosedDoors.pdf, 7 (accessed 4/16/15).

[37] Brian F. Martin, *Invincible: The 10 Lies You Learn Growing Up with Domestic Violence and the Truths to Set You Free* (New York, NY: Perigee, 2014), 224.

[38] Sonja Lyubomirsky, *The Myths of Happiness: What Should Make You Happy But Doesn't, What Shouldn't Make You Happy But Does* (New York, NY: Penguin Books, 2013), 79.

[39] http://www.carolineabbott.com/get-help/.

[40] Karyl McBride, *Will I Ever Be Good Enough? Healing the Daughters of Narcissistic Mothers* (New York, NY: Free Press, 2008), 135-137.

[41] Tracy, *Mending the Soul,* 145.

[42] Tracy, *Mending the Soul,* 136.

[43] Eleanor D. Payson, M.S.W., *The Wizard of Oz and Other Narcissists: Coping with the One-Way Relationship in Work, Love and Family* (Royal Oak, MI: Julian Day Publications), 80.

[44] Tracy, *Mending the Soul,* 143-156.

[45] Tracy, *Mending the Soul,* 150-51.

[46] American Psychiatric Association, *Diagnostic and Statistical Manual of Mental Disorders* (5th ed.) (American Psychiatric Association, 2013).

[47] Karyl McBride, *Will I Ever Be Good Enough? Healing the Daughters of Narcissistic Mothers* (New York, NY: Free Press, 2008), 151.

[48] Mohamed Mubarak Al Mazrouel, Tate Taylor (2011) *The Help* (USA: Walt Disney Pictures).

CHAPTER SIX

[49] Grief.com: "Because Love Never Dies," http://grief.com/the-five-stages-of-grief/ (accessed 4/16/15).

[50] Check out this website for emergency phone numbers for countries around the world: http://www.911dispatch.com/911/911_world.html (accessed 4/16/15).

[51] Emily Avagliano, *Dating After Trauma: How to Find the Love of Your Life After Experiencing an Abusive Relationship, Rape or Sexual Abuse* (Bad Kitty Print Shoppe: USA, 2013), 16.

[52] Emily Avagliano, *Dating After Trauma,* 64.

[53] Emily Avagliano, *Dating After Trauma,* 65–74.

[54] EMDR Institute, Inc., "What is EMDR?", http://emdr.com/what-is-emdr/ (accessed 10/6/15).

CHAPTER SEVEN

55 Lundy Bancroft, *When Dad Hurts Mom: Helping Your Children Heal the Wounds of Witnessing Abuse* (New York, NY: Berkley Books, 2004), 65.

56 Lundy Bancroft, *When Dad Hurts Mom*, 64.

57 Lundy Bancroft, "Assessing Risk to Children from Batterers," http://www.lundy-bancroft.com/articles/assessing-risk-to-children-from-batterers (accessed 4/15/15).

58 Lundy Bancroft, *When Dad Hurts Mom*, 269-270.

59 Jim Weidmann and Kurt Bruner, *An Introduction to Family Nights: Family Night Tool Chest* (Colorado Springs, CO: Victor Books, 1997).

60 Lundy Bancroft, *When Dad Hurts Mom*, 274-278.

61 Scott Brown, *How to Negotiate with Kids . . . Even When You Think You Shouldn't: Seven Essential Skills to End Conflict and Bring More Joy into Your Family* (New York, NY: Penguin Putnam, Inc:, 2004).

62 Lundy Bancroft, *When Dad Hurts Mom*, 304–305, 307-308.

63 Johnston, Walters, & Olesen, "Is it Alienating Parenting, Role Reversal or Child Abuse? A Study of Children's Rejection of a Parent in Child Custody Disputes," The Hayworth Press, 2005. https://www.ncjrs.gov/App/publications/abstract.aspx-?ID=234543 (accessed 4/30/15).

64 Lundy Bancroft, *When Dad Hurts Mom*, 246.

65 Lundy Bancroft, *When Dad Hurts Mom*, 247.

66 Daniel G. Saunders, Ph.D., Kathleen C. Faller, Ph.D., Richard M. Tolman, Ph.D. "Child Custody Evaluators' Beliefs About Domestic Abuse Allegations: Their Relationship to Evaluator Demographics, Background, Domestic Violence Knowledge and Custody-Visitation Recommendations" https://www.ncjrs.gov/pdffiles1/nij/grants/238891.pdf (accessesd 4/30/15).

67 Caroline Abbott, "Hope for the Family Court System," May 2014, http://www.carolineabbott.com/2014/05/hope-for-the-family-court-system/ (accessed 4/30/15).

68 Lundy Bancroft, *When Dad Hurts Mom*, Chapters 11, 12, and 13.

CHAPTER EIGHT

69 Bill Eiliff, with Tim Grissom, *Forgiveness: Healing the Harbored Hurts of Your Heart*, (North Little Rock, Arkansas: The Summit Church, 1998), 7.

70 Bill Elliff and Tim Grissom, *Forgiveness*, 9-10.

71 Bill Elliff and Tim Grissom, *Forgiveness*, 16-24.

72 Bill Elliff and Tim Grissom, *Forgiveness*, 20.

73 Tracy, *Mending the Soul*, 192-193.

74 Tracy, *Mending the Soul*, 193.

75 WebMD.com: "What Are the Symptoms of Stress?", http://www.webmd.com/

balance/stress-management/stress-symptoms-effects_of-stress-on-the-body?page=2 (accessed 4/15/15).

[76] Merriam-Webster Dictionary: http://www.merriam-webster.com/dictionary/ restitution (accessed 4/15/15).

[77] Timothy and Kathy Keller, *The Meaning of Marriage: Facing the Complexities of Commitment with the Wisdom of God* (New York, NY: Riverhead Books, 2013) 44.

[78] K-LOVE radio station, http://www.klove.com/: 1-800-525-LOVE (5683).

[79] Neil T. Anderson, *The Bondage Breaker: Overcoming Negative Thoughts, Irrational Feelings, Habitual Sins* (Eugene, OR: Harvest House Publishers, 2006).

[80] Charitie L. Bancroft, "Before the Throne of God Above," Capitol CMG Publishing, 1863, License number 560008.

CHAPTER NINE

[81] Joshua Harris, *I Kissed Dating Goodbye: A New Attitude Toward Romance and Relationships* (Colorado Springs, CO: Multnomah Publishers, 1997).

[82] Joshua Harris, *I Kissed Dating Goodbye*, 100.

[83] Joshua Harris, *I Kissed Dating Goodbye*, 101.

[84] Kate McVeigh, *Single and Loving It: Living Life to the Fullest* (Tulsa OK: Harrison House, 2003) 89.

[85] Kate McVeigh, *Single and Loving It*, 90.

[86] Caroline Abbott "We Are God's Bride," September 2015 http://www.carolineabbott.com/2015/09/we-are-gods-bride/.

[87] Kate McVeigh, *Single and Loving It*, 5-6.

[88] Joshua Harris, *I Kissed Dating Goodbye*, 51.

[89] Kate McVeigh, *Single and Loving It*, 128.

[90] Family Facts.org, "Four in 10 Children are Born to Unwed Mothers," 2011, http://www.familyfacts.org/charts/205/four-in-10-children-are-born-to-unwed-mothers (accessed 4/15/15).

[91] Joshua Harris, *Boy Meets Girl: Say Hello to Courtship* (Colorado Springs, CO: Multnomah Publishers, 2005) 26-27.

[92] Wikipedia, The Free Encyclopedia, http://en.wikipedia.org/wiki/Running_the_gauntlet (accessed 4/15/15).

[93] Emily Avagliano, *Dating After Trauma*, 112.

[94] Emily Avagliano, *Dating After Trauma*, 109.

[95] Emily Avagliano, *Dating After Trauma*, 116.

[96] Emily Avagliano, *Dating After Trauma*, 116-120.

CHAPTER TEN

97 http://www.carolineabbott.com/get-help/.

98 Emerson Eggerichs, *Love & Respect: The Love She Most Desires, the Respect He Desperately Needs* (Nashville, TN: Thomas Nelson, 2004).

99 See http://www.desiringgod.org/messages/husbands-who-love-like-christ-and-the-wives-who-submit-to-them for John Piper's sermon on June 11, 1989 about submission, (accessed 10/6/15).

100 Kaiser, Jr., "Correcting Caricatures: The Biblical Teaching on Women," http://http://walterckaiserjr.com/women.html, (accessed 10/6/15).

101 Dr. Henry Cloud and Dr. John Townsend, *Boundaries*, 161-162.

102 Dr. Cloud, *Boundaries*, 59.

103 Timothy and Kathy Keller, *The Meaning of Marriage: Facing the Complexities of Commitment with the Wisdom of God* (New York, NY:Riverhead Books, 2011), 149.

104 John M. Gottman, Ph.D and Nan Silver, *The Seven Principles for Making Marriage Work: A Practical Guide from the Country's Foremost Relationship Expert* (New York, NY: Harmony Books, 2015).

CHAPTER ELEVEN

105 *The Hiding Place*. Director James F. Collier. Performers Julie Harris, Jeannette Clift George. World Wide Pictures, 1975.

106 Andrew Murray, "I Am Here by God's Appointment," /http://justonemore.info/2011/01/i-am-here-by-god's-appointment (accessed 4/15/15).

107 Dillow, *Calm My Anxious Heart,* 180-184.

108 John Piper, "Don't Waste Your Cancer," March 3, 2006 http://www.crosswalk.com/faith/spiritual-life/don't-waste-your-cancer-1383847.html (accessed 10/6/15).

109 Jeff Rosenau, *Building Bridges Not Walls, Learning to Dialogue in the Spirit of Christ* (Colorado Springs, CO: NavPress, 2003). Note, this book has been rewritten and is now called: *When Christians Act Like Christians: God's Call to Christlike Civility* (Centennial, CO: Jeff Rosenau, 2010). http://www.christlikedialogue.org/small-group-study/when-christians-act-christians/ (accessed 10/6/15).

110 Go to the author's Get Help page for a list of books about domestic violence: http://www.carolineabbott.com/get-help/.

111 National Coalition Against Domestic Violence, http://www.ncadv.org (accessed 10/6/15).

112 Phillip Yancey, *The Question That Never Goes Away*, 80.

APPENDIX B

113 The National Domestic Violence Hotline, "Abuse Defined: Warning Signs and Red Flags," http://www.thehotline.org/is-this-abuse/abuse-defined/ (accessed 10/6/15).

CPSIA information can be obtained at www.ICGtesting.com
Printed in the USA
BVOW06s1636021115

425050BV00005B/9/P